Real Estate Investor Goddess

noun I \ˈriːəl ɪˈsteɪt ɪnˈvɛstə ˈɡɑdəs

1. A woman who pleasurably invests in real estate to build wealth, create the lifestyle she desires, and leave a property and community better than she finds it.

2. A gorgeous creature who unapologetically seeks to own the world, and who makes the world better as a result.

The Real Estate Investor Goddess Handbook:
Everything You Need to Know to Invest In Real Estate
Like a Goddess

Copyright © 2017 Monick Paul Halm

Published by Halm Style LLC

realestateinvestorgoddesses@gmail.com

ISBN-13: 978-0-6480154-2-0

ISBN-10: 0-6480154-2-4

The Real Estate Investor Goddess
HANDBOOK

EVERYTHING YOU NEED TO KNOW TO INVEST IN REAL ESTATE LIKE A GODDESS

Join the Real Estate Investor Goddesses Facebook Community

Share your testimonials, comments, questions, breakthroughs, successes and more.
For updates and The Real Estate Investor Goddesses news, LIKE our page at
www.facebook.com/RealEstateInvestorGoddesses

ALSO

Receive your special BONUSES for buying this book!
Access Multiple Free Gifts from Monick Halm and others.
Go to **www.RealEstateInvestorGoddesses.com**

Or send an email to
info@realestateinvestorgoddesses.com
With "Gifts" in the subject.

Praise for the *Real Estate Investor Goddess Handbook*

"This book is amazing. I swear, I've invested in real estate my whole life, and I learned more from 4 chapters of this book than I have from anything else!!!"

Barbara Stanny, bestselling author of *Prince Charming Isn't Coming: How Women Get Smart About Money, Overcoming Underearning* and *Sacred Success*

"Just when you thought the world couldn't use another book about real estate investing, Monick Halm finds a way to combine inspiration and education into an easy-to-read, actionable, practical, tactical guide to getting it done in the real world. This book is just like Monick … smart, fun, and action-oriented. And men will love it too!"

Russell Gray, Co-host of The Real Estate Guys™ Radio

"Monick has written a book about real estate investing that is not just actionable; it is also joyful. Few investors of either gender are willing to be as transparent and honest about their successes, failures, and sources of inspiration and education as Monick. This is quite certainly among the most enjoyable real estate reads I've ever encountered."

Carole VanSickle Ellis, Co-founder of the Self-Directed Investor Society and founder of SDI Women

"Monick Halm has created a true go-to guide for becoming a savvy, successful and smart real estate investor. She breaks things down into tools and strategies that are easy to grasp, motivating and inspiring for the reader to take action. I highly recommend this winning book!"

Kim Somers Egelsee, #1 best selling author of *Living The Ten+Life*

"Get on the fast track! Ladies (and gentlemen), you no longer have an excuse not to be investing in real estate. In this quick but thorough read, Monick answers the questions you have, and the ones you didn't know to ask. If you're ready to create serious wealth through real estate, read this book now!"

Robert Helms, Real Estate Investor, Developer and Host of The Real Estate Guys™ Radio & Television Programs

"As a how-to guide, this book contains practical information and straightforward strategies anyone can use to successfully invest in real estate."

Amanda Han, CPA and author of *The Book On Tax Strategies for the Savvy Real Estate Investor*

"If you want to shape your financial future with confidence, this book is for you. It provides great advice on generating real wealth and is a must read for any aspiring goddess."

Paula Brooks, founder, www.FinancialFreedomFaster.com

"With over 25 years in real estate investing I recognize the need and value of Monick's book. It's informative, easy to understand and a sound plan that anyone can follow. Based on a real life fascinating story, it's priceless for women who want to invest in their fabulous future!"

Desiree Doubrox, Founder/CEO, An Empowered Woman, Speaker, Producer and Publisher of Let's Talk Success and Founder/CEO of HomWork.

"Monick offers "real-world" advice that's useful for any woman (or man) who wishes to build wealth through real estate. This book offers lessons from the trenches that you can use to confidently march forward on your own investing path."

Kathy Fettke, CEO and co-founder of the Real Wealth Network, host of The Real Wealth Show, and author of *Retire Rich With Rentals*

Dedications

To my darling husband and real estate business partner, Peter Halm. Thank you for being my biggest cheerleader and my best friend.

To my incredible kids India, Teo, and Aliza - thank you for being my inspiration and also my teachers. You amaze me constantly.

To my wonderful mom and dad. In the parent lottery, I won the jackpot. You are the best, most supportive parents a girl could ever imagine. And to my siblings - Marc, Chris and Cookie. I also won the jackpot with you. Thanks for your amazing friendship and support. Thanks for also bringing my wonderful niece, nephews and sisters-in-law into my life.

To Denise Cooper, thanks for instantly getting my vision and co-creating the Real Estate Investor Goddesses with me.

To my editor Carole VanSickle Ellis - thank you for always being so supportive and helping make this book a much more beautiful and easy read.

To my teachers and mentors Kyle Wilson, Robert Helms, Russell Gray, Bob "The Godfather" Helms, Brad Sumrok, Barbara Stanny, and Regena Thomashauer - thank you for your immense generosity, and the inspiration you show as you walk your talk.

To my fellow Real Estate Investor Goddesses. Thank you for your willingness to be divine and to own the world!

Table of Contents

Introduction

"Real estate investing even on a very small scale,
remains a tried and true means of building
an individual's cash flow and wealth."
~Robert Kiyosaki, author of *Rich Dad, Poor Dad*

Welcome to the Real Estate Investor Goddesses Handbook!

My name is Monick Halm. I'm the co-founder of Real Estate Investor Goddesses (REIG). At REIG, we help women get successfully invested in real estate so they can build wealth, create the lifestyle they desire, and make a massive difference on the planet.

I'm also a wife, mama of three great kids, and a real estate investor with over 1,000 rental doors. My husband and I currently own duplexes, a mobile home park, and apartment buildings in 5 states. With the exception of two of these doors, we acquired the other 1000+ in the last 12 months.

I wasn't born with a silver spoon in my mouth. We always had a roof over our heads, but growing up I do remember a time or two when my dad was unemployed and we had to go on food stamps to have enough to eat. I also never inherited anything from anyone or won the lottery. Nor did I marry rich.

I built this real estate portfolio by myself and with my husband using the steps I'm going to share with you in this book.

How's your financial life?

So many people, women especially, are working hard every day earning wages at jobs and trying to make ends meet. Can you relate to the following statements?

* You are working hard and have relatively little to show for it. You are trading your time for money and struggling to find the free time to spend with your family. You would like to travel, to write that book you've been dying to write, or to just generally live the lifestyle you desire, but you cannot do those things and also *fund* those things.

* You are not sure how you're going to be able to pay for your retirement. Maybe you have some funds tucked away, but you're not sure the money will outlast you - especially if we go through another economic downturn and the market crashes again.

* You want to leave something for your kids: some financial resources they can rely on. It would be nice to be like Warren Buffett and leave your kids "enough so that they can do whatever they want, but not so much that they won't do anything."

* You work hard *all the time* but things seem to be getting worse instead of better. The cost of living has increased, but your wages haven't been rising enough to keep up. You are working harder and harder with less and less to show for it.

* You feel like you're on a hamster wheel, running and running and not making any progress toward your goals.

What if there's a better way to financial health and wealth?

There is another way of thinking about and using your money:

Don't work *for* your money. Put your money to work for you

While you're sleeping, traveling, spending time with your family or friends, your money can be invested in such a way that it's making YOU more money.

Instead of thinking of a dollar as something you work for, spend, and then have to work more for, what if you used each dollar bill as a seed that can be planted?

When planted well, your money can turn into a "money tree" that regularly delivers you money-fruit. You can regularly reap the harvest and plant some of those extra dollar bills until you've created a money orchard. When you have a large enough money orchard you will no longer have to trade your time for money. You can just tend to your money trees and enjoy the harvest.

That is financial freedom!

Real Estate Investing is the best way I've found to create a money orchard. It is one of the greatest ways to build wealth.

You plant your money into the right property and by putting in tenants they are paying the bills (mortgage, taxes, utilities, etc.) you are able to reap more dollars to boot.

Real estate investing gives you lifestyle freedom

Once the property is bought and tenants are installed, the property is making you money while you sleep or go on vacation. This occurs 24/7 without you having to do much work. When you have enough of these properties working so that your passive income from real estate exceeds your job, you can "retire" from working. You only work if you want to.

Real estate can give you a lasting legacy

When you build a money orchard that is something you can leave to your children or to charity. Land and property are gifts that can keep on giving for generations.

Real estate can give you regular cash flow

You can invest in real estate that cash flows from Day One (from the first day of your investment, your tree is delivering you fruit). It can cash flow in a way that almost no other investment does. This (and other strategies we will talk about in the book) allows you to more quickly and easily take your money seeds and plant more trees.

AND real estate gives you amazing tax benefits

The U.S. federal government has decided to reward real estate investment through certain great tax benefits.[1] Some of these are such that even though you can be making MORE money because of your real estate investment, you will owe LESS in taxes.

Something You Should Know:

I didn't grow up knowing any of this. I fell into real estate investment almost by accident.

I didn't know anything about real estate investing. I didn't know why someone would want to do it, or that it was even an option for me.

I was taught that you work hard in school, go to the best college (and in my case law school) you can, and then get the best job you can.

I was taught to trade time for money, but get the best job you can so that you're making the most amount of money per hour. It's not bad advice if you're money paradigm is that to make money, you

---

[1] I am based in the United States, so I will focus on United States tax law, but many other countries have similar incentives for property ownership. If you live outside of the US, please check with your local accountant/tax preparer to find out what benefits may apply to you.

need to get a job. The only thing I was taught about real estate was to buy your own home.[2]

So that's what I did. I worked hard in school; I went to Columbia Law School, and then I got a job working in a big law firm in Los Angeles. I was young, single, and making a good 6-figure salary. I was miserable in my job, but that's a different story for a different book.

After a few years of working and saving, I decided it was time to buy a house. It was Los Angeles in 2005, and we were getting toward the top of the bubble. Even though I had a 6-figure salary, it was hard to get a house I could afford in a neighborhood I wanted to live in.

A good friend of mine who also wanted to buy a house but was stymied by the high prices suggested that we buy something together. He suggested we buy a duplex and each live in one side of it.

I readily agreed. We'd been roommates together in law school and in Argentina. He was and still is one of my best friends. I knew I could live with him and that we would be successful business partners as well.

We ended up finding a beautiful home that we both fell in love with. Unlike our original vision of one property with two equal spaces that each one of us would inhabit, our dream house had one unit that was substantially larger and more attractive to live in than the other.

Instead of one of us living in the less desirable unit, we decided that we would each take a bedroom in the bigger unit and rent out the top unit. There was also a converted garage in the back that we were able to rent out. We moved in, got tenants for the

---

[2] For those of you who are familiar with Robert Kiyosaki's book *Rich Dad, Poor Dad* you know that despite what the banks say, a house you live in is not an "asset" in the Rich Dad way of thinking. An asset is something that puts money into your pocket, not one that takes money out.

converted garage and the upstairs duplex. All of a sudden, we were landlords.

And I realized something — being a landlord had some definite benefits! These tenants were paying the mortgage! I still owed a little bit at the end of every month, but I owed a whole heck of a lot less than I otherwise would have if I owned the place by myself or if I had continued renting.

On top of that I got to take mortgage and other tax deductions that resulted in even better savings. I was in the highest tax bracket so owning this property made a BIG DIFFERENCE in my final tax bill. I got to keep a lot more from Uncle Sam.

I liked this real estate thing!

I didn't yet know to grow an orchard, but I had planted a pretty great tree. (And don't worry. I'll share more in Chapter 3 about how I went from having those two rental units to more than 1,000 rental doors today. 99.9 percent of which I acquired in the past 12 months.)

It was when I realized that my tenants were paying my mortgage *and* I was saving money on my taxes that I realized real estate was a great way to go.

Most people would agree that real estate is an incredible wealth-builder. Oddly, however, most people are not investing in real estate and, of those that are, a very small percentage of them are women.

Which begs the question:

Why aren't more women investing in real estate?

There are three main reasons I believe more women aren't investing in real estate:

1) **Many simply have not considered the incredible advantages of real estate, or that they could ever participate as a real estate investor**

   Perhaps they haven't considered that there is an option for creating income other than trading their time for money. Or maybe they just think it's something that "very rich" people do, and it's not something they could ever afford.

2) **They understand real estate investing in the abstract, but do not know how to apply those concepts to their own work or investing**

   They understand the concepts of real estate investment, but they don't know how to do it. They don't know what steps to take, or where to go in order to gain the necessary knowledge.

3) **Last but certainly not least, they understand how it works, but they're afraid they're going to lose money**

   They have heard of people making lots of money in real estate, but they've also heard of people losing lots of money in real estate. They're afraid they're going to "lose their panties" and be worse off than before.

In this book we are going to address all of these issues.

You will learn:

• **All of the incredible advantages of real estate**

   By the time we're done, you will fully understand exactly what those advantages are are and how *you* can take advantage of *them.*

- **Precisely how real estate investing works**

  You'll be 100-percent confident in your knowledge of the specific steps you need to take to succeed and the specific things you should avoid at all costs. You'll be crystal clear about how to successfully invest in a way that's uniquely feminine and takes advantages of a woman's unique gifts to be successful.

- **How other women have succeeded, beyond their and your wildest dreams, in this industry**

  Throughout the book we are going to share inspirational stories of women who are killing it in real estate. They're women like you and me who found about how to build a money orchard through real estate and did it. We're going to share how so that you are inspired and know that if they did it you can too!

The Real Estate Investor Goddess Handbook is designed to give you the basics to successfully invest in a real estate deal that's right for you.

This book shares a formula calibrated to get you *pleasurably* invested in properties and living the real estate investor lifestyle you desire.

I want you to be a success!

As a Real Estate Strategy Mentor, certified Money Mastery Coach, Neuro-Linguistic Practitioner (NLP) and Success Coach, and as an observer of this process, I have seen many investors who do incredibly well, and hundreds more who *want* to accomplish but end up doing very little.

Let me share with you some important steps to make sure that this process is a success for you.

Here's how to be successful with the Real Estate Investor Goddess Handbook

These steps are important because while none of the lessons in this book are in and of themselves anywhere near impossible, they will require you to take some bold steps and possibly make some changes. Change itself can be difficult. These 7 tips will help make that change a bit easier.

1. Make the process joyful

Set up a special time and atmosphere for working through the *Real Estate Investor Goddess Handbook* and your real estate dreams. Find a quiet and peaceful corner, play your favorite relaxing music, and make yourself a delicious cup of tea or hot chocolate before you begin to dive into each chapter.

Remember that joyful journeys lead to joyful results.

2. Find a friend/accountability partner to read this book with/get on the investment path with you.

Encourage them to get the book and work through the exercises together. Discuss your challenges and wins, and support each other as you create your orchard.

We have tried to make the steps in this book as easy to implement as possible, but making any change to your normal ways of doing things is not easy. Having someone to help support you (and who you can mutually support) will greatly increase your chances for success.

If you want more support and updated lessons join our Real Estate Investor Goddesses Wealth Builders Online Group. In this online membership program you will find a supportive community, up to date lessons, and live webinars where you can have access to me and other experts in real estate investing and related fields.

Go to **www.RealEstateInvestorGoddesses.com** to register and find out more.

3. Cut yourself some slack

The goal is progress, not perfection. There WILL be days when it feels like you are not making any progress or have even moved backwards. It might feel like you're failing. The trick is to fail forward. To learn from setbacks and to keep at it. Again, having an accountability partner and supportive community will help with this.

4. Commit to forward movement

You may not be able to do as much or as quickly as you want, but commit to taking even one baby step of forward movement daily.

5. Speak yourself into success

Just for the duration of your time reading this book (or your entire life if you're so inclined), cut out talk of failure, lack, and limitation. Instead of "I don't have the money," say "I am resourceful and can find the resources I need to make this happen." Instead of "This is too hard, I can't do it," say "This is challenging me, but I'm up to this challenge."

The words you use make a HUGE difference in your success.

6. **Commit to Your Success**

A contract you make with yourself is a powerful motivator. I have created a contract that you can print out and fill in to fortify your resolve.

You can access this contract at

www.RealEstateInvestorGoddesses.com.

I highly encourage you to get this contract ASAP.

Otherwise, you may be shortchanging yourself.

Chapter One – The 4 Myths of Real Estate Investing

"There are myths that plague the world of real estate investment. Some of these do no real harm, but others prevent investors from reaching their full potential. Worse, they can cause missed opportunities and poor decisions when real estate investors buy into misconceptions about the industry."
~Chris Clothier, Memphis Invest

Recognizing and challenging any limiting beliefs about real estate is the first step in becoming a successful real estate investor Goddess. So many women severely limit what they accomplish or worse, they *don't even get started,* because they believe one of the following myths:

Myth 1: You need to have a lot of money or time to invest in real estate

A lot of women I speak to say, "I'd love to invest in real estate and I will as soon as I've got more money." Or "I'd love to invest, but I don't have time to find a property or be a landlord."

Women think they're limited because they have limited resources. I thought the same thing.

My husband and I were searching for a 4-unit property to buy in Los Angeles and were stuck finding the right investment because we were only thinking that we had to use our own capital, credit, or available time.

Tony Robbins says, *"There's no lack of resources, just a lack of resourcefulness."* When we became educated about the possibilities out there and realized the many creative ways we could partner with others to become investors, we became much more resourceful.

The truth is that you **don't** need to have a lot of money and you **don't** need to have a lot of time. You don't even have to use any of your own money! You just need the education and creativity to become more resourceful.

Myth 2: You have to do it yourself

This is a big myth in real estate. Not only do you not have to do it by yourself, if you want to grow an orchard it's almost impossible to do it by yourself.

If you limit yourself to your own capital, credit, and time, you could accomplish quite a bit but eventually you will hit a wall. If you partner with others and utilize OPM (Other People's Money) or OPT (Other People's Time), there's no limit to what you can do.

If my husband and I were just trying to invest by ourselves, we might have acquired a four-unit multifamily building, a "fourplex," (not bad), but by partnering with others we were able to become part owners in over 1000 units. In certain cases, we were able to get an ownership stake by using none of our own money (it was all OPM). And in other cases, we just put in some money and someone else found the deal and is managing it for us. All we do is enjoy the quarterly checks (it's all OPT).

Myth 3: You have to start small

Most people start out buying a duplex or a single-family home to rent out. I did. It's common, but that's definitely not where you need to start or even where it's most prudent to start.

One of my mentors, Brad Sumrok, started out with a 32-unit building. He learned about the beauty of leverage and purchased an apartment building first. He was able to turn around that building and buy another and another. Within 3 years he'd earned enough to be able to "retire" from a six-figure management job. His passive income became greater than his paycheck. Now he teaches others, like my husband and me, how to retire from the rat race through investing in apartment buildings.

Starting bigger has some definite benefits. One of the best things about having a bigger property is that you can hire a property manager (usually for small properties, property management is cost prohibitive). When you have a property manager, you have someone else who deals with leasing out to tenants, handling evictions, fixing toilets, receiving 3 a.m. phone calls for keys, etc. You actually can spend less time on a bigger building and leave yourself more bandwidth for planting more trees in your money orchard.

We will talk more about the beauty of leverage that you get from bigger properties in the next chapter.

Myth 4: Investing in stocks is safer/better investment than real estate

This whopper is generally perpetrated by stock brokers or other financial professionals that get paid to put you into these types of investments.

First, it's important to know that any investment has risk. It is possible to lose money in real estate just like it's possible to lose money in the stock market.

That being said, a well-educated real estate buyer who buys *a cash-flowing property* [3], is much more likely to make money than a stock market investor.

Real Estate has at least seven major benefits that make it a better investment option.

In the next chapter, we will share these many benefits. Make sure to read them, so you don't miss out on taking advantage of them.

---

[3] A cash-flowing property is a property that makes money after all expenses are paid. I personally recommend investing in properties that are cash-flowing from day one.

Chapter Two – The 7 Main Benefits of Real Estate Investing

"Ninety percent of all millionaires become so through owning real estate. More money has been made in real estate than in all industrial investments combined. The wise young man or wage earner of today invests his money in real estate."
~Andrew Carnegie, industrialist and billionaire

Real Estate has many benefits for investors, but most people are unaware of all of these benefits.

It's important to know and understand the benefits so that you can fully take advantage of them.

The 7 Main Benefits of Real Estate are:

1. Cash Flow Opportunities

Tenants pay rent. After expenses, what you have is monthly, recurring mostly passive cash flow. This is a benefit that most real estate investors expect and understand.

Cash flow does not happen for the vast majority of stock holders.

Typically, you only make money when you sell the stock after the stock value has gone up.

2. Appreciation

Sometimes properties lose value, but over the long term the value of real estate will nearly always go up. This happens while the loan is being paid down. The advantage of this is that as your property gains value or equity your net worth increases.

Property values generally appreciate in 2 ways - (1) increase in value due to the market, and (2) forced increase in value due to making targeted improvements."

For our apartment buildings, we work toward both types of appreciation. We bought in a market where we expect market values to rise over the next few years.

We also bought a building that was operating under market because the apartments were old and in bad shape and the previous owners were unable to charge market rents. By rehabbing the apartments, we were able to start charging more rent and increase the value of the building. **This is called "forced appreciation."**

When we sell the property in approximately 5 years, we can also recoup any appreciation in the market that may happen because neighboring properties are also selling for more.

3. U.S. Federal Tax Benefits

There are many tax benefits to owning property. Many people aren't aware of them, but they're one of the best benefits to owning real estate. In the section below I'll lay some of them out for you.[4]

Depreciation

The first major tax benefit is a beautiful thing called "depreciation." Depreciation allows you to deduct a portion of property values (buildings and improvements) from income over a period of time. This gives you a "phantom expense" that you can write off your taxes.

Depreciation is not taken on the land, but it is taken on buildings/ physical structures attached to it. Even though a building will usually gain value over time (see appreciation above), the government sees buildings as *losing* value over time.

For residential property and improvements, the U.S. government has a depreciation time of 27.5 years. For commercial property and improvements, it's 39 years.

Essentially, this means that the government expects it to take 27.5 years for your residential investment property to be worth absolute zero, and 39 years for your commercial property. They divide that lost value by the designated time span, and the resulting value is the amount of annual depreciation that you can write off each year.

Let me give you an example: let's say you purchase a piece of residential property for $100,000 and the land it sits on is valued at $25,000. Assuming your closing costs are $2,000, here's what would happen:

$100,000 (purchase price)
+ $2,000 (closing costs)
_____

---

[4] Note, I'm not a CPA or Tax Professional. This is just information I've learned over my travels as a real estate investor. Please check with your own tax professional when doing your taxes.

$102,000 (total acquisition cost)

– $25,000 (subtract lot value)

$77,000 (amount to be depreciated)

$77,000/27.5 = $2,800 per year!

In this example, one rental house purchased for $100,000 would yield an annual tax write-off (depreciation expense) of $2,800. **If you had 10 of these, you'd be able to write off 10 times this amount, or $28,000.**

It's possible to get to a point where your depreciation expense exceeds your income and you actually could report that *you lost money*! This is how many professional landlords and seasoned buy-and-hold investors lower their taxes substantially.

The other nice benefit of depreciation is that you get to take depreciation off of the **entire value** of the property, even though in all likelihood you only paid for a portion of it since most investors, like any other home-buyer, tend to finance their properties when they purchase them.

Let's say you bought that $100,000 property above with a 10% down payment. In other words, someone else (the bank) has paid 90% of the value. You only personally paid $10,000, but you can still take depreciation of $2800 or 28% of your investment. That's a huge benefit!

Be aware, however: it's not all free money though - at least not forever. When you sell the property, the IRS will want to get paid back with something called "Depreciation Recapture."

If you own that $100,000 property for 10 years and have taken $28,000 of depreciation, upon sale the IRS will recapture that amount and charge long-term capital gains tax on it.

"Capital gains taxes" are fees that the government charges when you sell investments that have increased substantially in value since you originally purchased them. These taxes are based on your income tax bracket and the type of investment that yielded the profit.

For real estate in 2016, the most you might have owed in capital gains taxes was around 25 percent of the profits. Fortunately, there are a number of ways to reduce or even eliminate these taxes on your real estate profits.

For starters, depreciation recapture is only applicable to the extent that you had a gain (or profit) on the sale of the property. So, if you sell that property for $120,000 and only have a $20,000 gain, the IRS will only recapture depreciation up to $20,000. In other words, the other $8,000 that you were able to use as depreciation will not be taxed because it did not make it into the equation upon sale of the property.

1031 Exchanges

There's another way to avoid capital gains altogether: a 1031 exchange.

The 1031 exchange is a legal tax strategy that many savvy real estate investors use to bypass depreciation recapture and other taxes upon the sale of a property.

It's named after the IRS tax code Section 1031, the statute governing it, and allows an individual to sell an asset, like a piece of property, and defer the capital gains taxes on the profits of that sale by purchasing new, higher priced property within a relatively short time period.

In other words, a real estate investor can use this tax code to sell a property and use the profit to buy a new one, and defer paying taxes until that next property is sold (unless, of course, they use another 1031 Exchange). It's a game of "kick the can" with taxes.

There are some limits some limits to this rule,[5] but if an investor can do a 1031 Exchange within those limits it can be very beneficial for the investor.

The Longer You Hold a Property, The Less You Will Pay in Taxes.

Real estate tax benefits are such that you can increase your income while still *decreasing* your tax burden. In other words, you can make more and still pay less in taxes. If you own a property for one year or less though (hello flippers), you will pay taxes at the normal income tax rate.

If you own a property for over a year, as most real estate investors do, then you will pay less in taxes or long-term capital gains. In fact, you can pay 0% capital gains tax for profits under $75,000!

Property Income Has a Different Treatment Than Other Self-Employment Income.

Another tax benefit to owning rental properties is that there is no self-employment tax on rental cash flow. Self-employed individuals must generally pay self-employment tax as well as

---

[5]The IRS has some pretty strict rules that govern the 1031 Exchange. These rules MUST be followed strictly, or the investor may lose the entire benefit and be forced to pay the tax. These rules are:

(1) The Exchange Must Be For a "Like-Kind Asset." In other words, you can't sell a primary residence and buy a Cardio Barre franchise. However, "like-kind" is a loosely defined term, so you could sell a rental house and buy an apartment, a piece of land, or a mobile home park.

(2) The Exchange Must Happen Within the Applicable Time Limits. After the sale of your property, the IRS requires that you identify the property you plan to buy within 45 days (you can identify three possible properties), and you must close on one property within 180 days.

(3) The Money Must Be Held in a Special Escrow Account. When you sell your property, you cannot touch the profit from the sale. Instead, you must use an intermediary who will hold onto the cash while you wait to close on the new deal. You can take out some of the profit; you'll just need to pay taxes on whatever you touch.

Tax Bracket for Married Individuals Filing Jointly - 2016		
Income Range	Tax Rate	Long Term Capital Gains Tax Rate
$0-$18,550	10%	0
$18,550 - $75,300	15%	0
$75,301 - $151,900	25%	15%
$151,900-$231,450	28%	15%
$231,451 - $413,350	33%	15%
$413,350 - $466,950	35%	15%
$466,951+	39.6%	20%

Data: IRS.gov

income tax, but if your employment involves owning rental properties, then you're in the clear! Obviously, check that out for your personal circumstances with your personal tax advisor.

Let's give an example — let's just say last year your next-door neighbor made $70,000 per year as a self-employed business owner. You also earned $70,000, but $50,000 of your income came from rents and the other $20,000 came from the profits of a property you sold.

Your neighbor's $70,000 was taxed at 15%, but she also had to pay 15% in self-employment tax. She's paying a total of 30% tax on her income.

You, on the other hand, paid $0 in taxes on the $20,000 in capital gains and no self-employment tax on any of your income. The only tax due was your 15% income tax on the $50k in rental income, but with all the deductions (including depreciation and the standard deductions), you ended up paying next to nothing, while your neighbor lost almost 1/3 of her income to the IRS!

Tax Deductions for Real Estate Investors

There are so many tax deductions that are available to real estate investors, and a lot of them are highly specific to your unique investment strategies. You will definitely need to work with an accountant to identify all of the options at your disposal. To give you an idea of what you can do once you start investing in real estate, I will highlight a couple of them here.

1) Mortgage interest and property taxes

Most investors and tax preparers are aware of the mortgage interest and property tax deductions. The mortgage interest deduction allows taxpayers who own property to reduce their taxable income by the amount of interest paid on the loan which is secured by the property.

Property taxes paid at closing when buying or selling a property, as well as taxes paid to your county or town's tax assessor (either directly or through a mortgage escrow account) on the assessed value of your property, may be deducted from your income tax for:

> Main Home
> Vacation homes
> Land
> Foreign property

In the case of rental or business property, the taxes *aren't* itemized deductions, but they can be claimed as an expense that offsets income.

2) "Grateful Deductions"

Fewer investors are aware of what my CPA and real estate tax expert, Amanda Han, author of *The Book On Tax Strategies for the Savvy Real Estate Investor*, calls "grateful deductions."

Not taking these deductions is the #1 mistake she sees most real estate investors make.

What Amanda calls "grateful expenses" are expenses that people are grateful to be able deduct because they're expenses that you'd have anyway, but because they are expenses that are "reasonable and ordinary" for real estate investment, they can be moved from the personal non-deductible bucket to the deductible bucket.

Examples of these "grateful expenses" are:

- cell phone
- computer
- home office
- travel costs
- car
- entertaining costs, such as dinner with potential investors
- education costs such as classes or books on personal development or real estate investment (like this one!)

How do you know if an otherwise personal expense should be classified as a legitimate business expense?

Amanda says you should ask yourself: "Would an ordinary real estate investor have this expense?" If the answer is yes, then you can deduct it.

Most people (even many accountants) don't realize this is possible, so they miss all these deductions. They don't claim the hundreds and sometimes thousands of dollars in deductions they could legally claim.

And the nice thing is these business deductions are not just for LLCs and Corporations. Even if you're a W2 employee doing real estate on the side, you can take advantage of these business deductions.

4. Leverage

The ability to leverage is one of the greatest benefits of real estate investment.

There are 3 ways to use leverage to enhance your real estate strategy and investment options:

a) You can leverage with money

This is by getting a mortgage and/or having investors invest with you. You leverage OPM to buy a property.

An example of how we leveraged money was when we invested in a 77-unit apartment building in Albuquerque, New Mexico.

We got a loan from a bank for 80% of the value of the building. We also partnered with other investors to pay the 20% of the down payment plus the rehab (the money we will need to upgrade the property).

We invested our time and leveraged other people's money to buy this property.

b) You can leverage with time

If you passively invest in projects, you can leverage other people's time.

The active investor will find the deal and manage it, while the passive investor provides the funding. You can invest in real estate while using OPT. If you're part of a syndication, you're also able to take advantage of OPM because you're piggy-backing off of all the other investors to get into the deal.

You are also leveraging time when you have property managers doing the work for you, and all you need to do is collect the profits each month.

All of these time-leveraging strategies give you more time while still putting your money to work in real estate.

c) You can leverage with other people's experience

If you're new and don't have experience, you can leverage the experience of others.

When we were just starting out we were able to leverage the experience of others to help us get in the door and get our properties.

Our next-door neighbor Lydia is a bad-ass real estate investor goddess. She is the vice president of an investment fund and has personally worked on over $1.5 billion worth of syndications.[6] She had done most of her syndications under the aegis of her employer and wanted to work on her own deals. She was incredibly busy with her job though.

We had more time available, but not her experience. We were able to do a lot of the leg work and she was able to (much more quickly than us) evaluate and underwrite deals.

We partnered with her and her husband to find deals. With her vast experience on our team resume it was very easy to open doors and get brokers/lenders to take us seriously.

We leveraged her experience to dramatically expand the breadth of our own knowledge while making money in real estate in the process.

---

[6] "Syndication" is a means of purchasing real estate with a pool of other investors.

d) You can leverage with the property itself

The more units you have the more leverage you have within the property itself.

If you have a single-family rental and you lose a tenant, your place is empty and you are losing money. You have zero income yet still have to pay the mortgage, insurance and property taxes.

If you have two units and you lose a tenant, you're still making 50% of your income. If you have 10 units, and you lose a tenant, you still have 90% of your income. If you have 100 units, and you lose one tenant you'll still have 99% of your income. You get the point.

Leverage also works in the positive. If you leverage a bigger property, small changes make a huge difference.

If you have a single-family home and are able to raise rent by $50 per month, you can make an extra $600 per year. If you have a 100-unit apartment building you raise rents $50/month that's $5k/month or $60k/year income. Furthermore, because the value of a 5+ unit is based off of net operating income, these increases will significantly increase the value of the property.

Lastly, when you have a larger place you have economies of scale that make it more cost effective to pay for professional property management. This means that you can have more tenants, but do less work (no fixing toilets for you!)

5. Principle Pay Down

As you pay down your mortgage (which is OPM) with interest, with each payment you pay back some principle and come closer and closer to owning the property free and clear. This is allowing you to build equity and wealth.

The doubly nice part about that is when you have a cash-flowing income property, your tenants are paying this down for you and helping your build your wealth and equity at the same time.

6. Re-finance

A re-finance is when you put in a new mortgage on a property. If your property has equity (from appreciation plus principal paid own), you can do a cash-out refinance (pull out some of the equity gained).

The best thing about a cash-out refinance is that it is not a taxable event. You have pulled out this income tax free.

A savvy investing Goddess will use this cash-out refinance to buy more income properties, and grow her orchard in that way.

This is what one of our Real Estate Investor Goddesses, Sarah May did. She and her husband saved up some money and put a down payment on a duplex. They rented it out and started cash flowing on that.

They were able to save up some more for another duplex. From there they did a cash-out refinance and bought another duplex. Then she just "rinsed and repeated."

When I interviewed her for this book, she had just closed on her 10th such income property, a fourplex, in the Denver Area where she lives. She and her husband did this in under 10 years.

And as of last year, they had created enough passive income from their real estate that she was able to "retire" from her 6-figure job as an engineer to be with their toddler full-time and to work on acquiring more real estate.

7. Real Estate is a "Feel-Good" Business

Having a business that simply "feels good" is particularly important to women. In a recent interview I did with Barbara Stanny, women and money expert, she said:

"Once a woman has enough to have food on the table, a roof over her head, and a mani-pedi every once in a while, she no longer is motivated by money. What motivates her is how to help others. It's a very different game. 'How can I help others and be richly rewarded?'"

If you invest according to the mission of the Real Estate Investor Goddesses, you can help others and be richly rewarded.

Our Mission is to invest in properties that enable us to:

• *Make a property and a community better than we found it*

• *Only engage in win-win transactions*

• *Ensure that everyone touched by our deals is uplifted and benefits*

If you make a property and community better than you find it, than you are benefiting the tenants and neighbors.

If you are engaging in win-win transactions, it benefits all involved. Sellers are happy and you're happy.

Everyone touched by your deal can be uplifted and benefited. Your income property is like a ripple of prosperity that spreads throughout the community. In every transaction the sellers, brokers, agents, property managers, other investors, and other service providers (lenders, accountants, contractors) are enriched.

And personally it feels good because while you are doing all this good you are making money passively (i.e., even while you sleep, go on vacation, etc., your properties are making you money). This gives you financial and TIME freedom.
Don't you feel good already?

Chapter Three – My Story

"If I can do this, so can you." ~Monick Halm

I want to share my story with you. This is a story that will resonate with you if you have had any of these challenges:

* You want to get started in real estate, but you are not quite sure where to start.

* Your real estate vision is big, but your bank account balance is too small to fund it.

* You have heard that real estate is a relationship game and you need a great team, but you don't know how to get into those relationships and/or where to start finding the right team.

* You know that you need to get educated on an investment before you invest, but you are not sure where and how to find information that's written in plain English.

* You are trying to find a real estate deal, but don't have the foggiest clue how to find one and aren't sure if it's a good one if you do find one.

* And last, but not least, you are finding the real estate investing world to be uber-masculine and it's just not turning you on.

If you relate to any of those, I hear you. I dealt with all of them. Here's my story of struggle...

My husband and I decided we wanted to get into multi-family real estate investment because we wanted to have some passive cash flow, build up some equity, and leave a legacy for our kids.

We started looking and asked our real estate agent to help us.

The real estate agent that had helped us get our single-family house knew nothing about investment property. Though she tried her best, she really was completely ignorant about what we needed to look for and alas, mostly so were we.

The commercial brokers who could have helped us were not interested in speaking to "small fries" who had no real experience in multi-family investing.

We were looking for a fourplex in Los Angeles where we live, and the prices were unbelievably high. It was really hard to find a deal where (a) we could even afford it and (b) where we'd be making any money.

I was incredibly frustrated and eventually despaired that we'd ever find anything.

Then, fate stepped in, as it often does when you're on the right path...

I met the man who would eventually become my mentor.

His name is Robert Helms and he's the co-host of the "Real Estate Guys Radio" podcast. He's also a real estate investor and developer with hundreds of millions of dollars' worth of deals under his belt.

A 10-minute conversation with him changed my life.

In that ten minutes I realized where I'd been going wrong.

First, we were looking in a market where the numbers didn't make any sense for what we were trying to do.

He told me: "Live where you want to live. Invest where the numbers make sense." I never thought of looking outside of the market where I live. That had been a huge mistake because my market was neither affordable nor landlord-friendly.

Second, we were not taking advantage of leverage.

Robert opened my mind to the idea that instead of trying to get one fourplex by ourselves, we could partner with a group of investors and get a 100-unit or 200-unit building. We could have a much bigger payout with less work and less risk.

Third, I realized I wasn't around people who were thinking big enough.

In my previous crowd, everyone thought getting a fourplex was a big deal. No one I knew would have conceived of investing in a 200-unit apartment building!

I decided right then and there, I wanted to be around folks who were thinking much bigger and to learn to think like them.

That night I went home and told my husband what I'd learned and about the next Real Estate Guys' syndication seminar in Phoenix. We signed up and bought our plane tickets.

We attended that event in January 2016. Since then we've attended a dozen other different real estate conferences all over the country, a real estate event in Belize, and a real estate investor cruise. We've joined two real estate mentorship groups. We have watched dozens of hours of training videos and read half a dozen books. We invested hundreds of hours and over $60,000[7] that year alone to learn how to successfully invest in real estate and it's paid off.

What we've learned and the community with which we've surrounded ourselves have really helped us to collapse time frames and increase cash flow and profits.

---

[7] Don't let that amount freak you out. I invested that much and then created Real Estate Investor Goddesses because I knew not many women would ever be able to do that. I invest an enormous amount of my time and money so that hopefully you won't have to.

Over the course of the past year we passively invested in a 320-unit property in Dallas and a 454-unit community in Atlanta, syndicated a 109-unit mobile home park, and a 77-unit building and a 51-unit building in Albuquerque, New Mexico. We are currently syndicating a 199-unit RV park in Lake Charles, Louisiana.

And we've accomplished all this for less money than we would have invested to buy that fourplex in Los Angeles.

I'm not sharing this to brag, but to show what is possible.

And all that was great. But…there was one big thing I noticed was largely missing from all the trainings I went to: the feminine presence.

I'd look around these rooms where I was learning incredibly valuable information and usually less than 10% of attendants were women!

There are relatively so few women in the real estate investment realm, and it is my desire to change that.

That desire led me to create the Real Estate Investor Goddesses.

We created an online membership community, blog and podcast that will help you quantum-leap into real estate investing at a fraction of the time and cost I did, and with a heightened dose of pleasure.

We know that many women who would love to learn this information do not have tens of thousands of dollars and hundreds of hours to invest in learning these concepts like I was blessed to.

Even if they do, many more simply do not desire to do so - especially in the uber-masculine way I was taught this information.

This book and the Real Estate Investor Goddess Online Membership Community was designed to help fix that. Find out more about it at **www.RealEstateInvestorGoddesses.com.**

Chapter Four – The Real Estate Investor Goddess Framework

"You don't have to be a genius or a visionary or even a college graduate to be successful. You just need a framework and a dream."
~Michael Dell

There is a 7-part framework you must follow to successfully invest like a Goddess. If any piece is missing, the structure will be unsound and your investment might not work.

For most people a real estate investment is the biggest investment they'll make in their lifetimes - you can win big, but if you don't follow the framework I'm going to share, you could lose big too.

The framework for a successful real estate investment is fairly simple — I envision it like the creation of a building.

Step 1 – Get the Right Education

When you're going to create a building, before you can even create the blueprint you need the right education. You need to be educated about architecture, building codes and safety.

Similarly, in real estate investing, **your first step is education**. You need to be educated about real estate investing in general - what to look for and what to look out for. The biggest mistake an investor can make is to invest in a deal they do not understand.

If you're uneducated you can invest in the wrong thing or possibly worse, you can miss out on the many opportunities to invest in the right thing and to build wealth.

I realize that I am preaching to the choir right now. You already understand the need for education or you probably wouldn't be reading this book. Do not allow this book to be the end of your education, however; this book must be just the beginning. Continue to be a student, because as Warren Buffett says "the best investment you can make is in yourself." This type of investment will always pay you back in spades.

Step 2 – Create Your Right Vision

The next step is to create a blueprint or plan. If you're making a blueprint for a building, the blueprint will be very different if the building is going to be a 2-bedroom house or a 100-story skyscraper.

Similarly in real estate investing, your plan, that is to say your vision and strategy for a successful real estate investment, must be tailored to your particular wants, needs and desires.

If you have the wrong blueprint, you're not going to make the right investment decisions for yourself.

In the next chapter - Chapter 5 - you will learn how to make a smart plan for your real estate investing that supports your desired life and lifestyle.

Step 3 – Build the Right Team

When erecting a house or building the first step is to create the foundation. In real estate investing, the foundation of any real estate deal is your team.

Real estate is a team sport. Depending on your deal you need a solid team of comprised of a realtor/broker, lender, insurance broker, property manager, contractor, CPAs, attorneys, mentors, and/or investing partners. If any member of your team is weak, you will have a weak foundation to build on and your investment may not work.

In Chapter 7, we will talk more about who you need on your team and what to look for to make sure you get the right team for you.

Step 4 – Find the Right Property Market

Once the foundation is set, the next step in the process of erecting a building is to create the frame. The frame has to be set correctly or the walls won't hang.

In real estate investing, that frame is the market. If you're investing in the wrong property market (for example, a market where no one wants to live), you could very well lose money.

You could have the most beautiful property, but if it's in a swamp you are very unlikely to have any tenants who want to live there.

On the other hand, what might be considered a shack in many other parts, set in the hottest part of hot market will be swooped up for top dollar.

I had a friend who lived in a 200-square-foot studio in the West Village in Manhattan for four years and paid over $900 a month for that tiny space in the 1990's! Now I'm sure some other tenant is currently paying double or triple what she paid for that space and considers themselves lucky to be able to do so. The owner of that studio has the good fortune (and the good sense) to have snapped up a property in a hot market when the "getting was good."

The trick is to find the right market and to buy in the right market cycle. We will show you how to figure out the right market and right market cycle in chapter 8.

Step 5 – Acquire the Right Property

After you have the frame set in a building, you next put up the walls. In real estate investing terms, this means finding the right property.

You want to make sure you're getting a property that's sound for a price that's sounder. If not, you're going to have cracks in your investment.

There are three aspects to getting the right property - the physical characteristic, the price, and the ownership situation. In Chapter 9, we'll show you how to assess each of these aspects to pick your perfect investment property.

Step 6 – Get the Right Financing

The next step in a building is to have a roof. The roof in investment terms is the financing. Without the right financing your building might soon be underwater.

In Chapter 10, we will talk about the different types of loans available - commercial or residential and how you can take advantage of this.

We will also talk about different creative ways you can get financing - from seller financing to gathering a group of investors together to purchase.

Step 7 – Add the "Goddess Secret Sauce"

After you have the house built it needs some paint and curb appeal. It has to be aesthetically pleasing or no one will want to live there.

In real estate investing, especially for a Goddess, the equivalent to "curb appeal" and a little basic beauty in your building is adding sisterhood, pleasure, and your intuitive guidance to the real estate investing process. This is the secret sauce.

It invites in magic and miracles.

In Chapter 11 we will talk about why these things are so important for women (it literally has to do with our physiology) and how you can ensure you incorporate these things into your real estate investing. Because who doesn't want magic and miracles? Quite frankly, a little dose of magic and miracles in your real estate investing can do wonders for your down-to-earth bottom line, and you'd be foolish not to invite that opportunity into your business and into your life.

Chapter Five – Your Right Education

"Real estate is truly the #1 greatest wealth builder, but it should not be taken lightly. With proper education, you can avoid the mistakes others have made, and learn from the strategies that work in any market cycle."
~Kathy Fettke, *Retire Rich With Rentals*

The first part of the framework is having the right education. Why is this important?

Education helps you avoid investing in the wrong things

The biggest mistake an investor can make is not understanding the investment they are making. There are two ways to lose money: invest in the wrong vehicle (for you) or invest in a bad vehicle. Both are the result of a lack of education. Without education, you will not be able to tell a good deal from a bad deal, or a good deal *for you* from a bad deal *for you*.

Just the other day, I had the pleasure of interviewing Barbara Stanny, author of the books *Secrets of Six-Figure Women, Overcoming Underearning, and Sacred Success* (among others).

Even though Barbara was the daughter of Richard Bloch, the "R" in H&R Block, and grew up very wealthy, she was never taught anything about money. Her father didn't think it was a woman's place to deal with money.

As a result of her father's attitude, she grew up wealthy and blissfully ignorant, and married a man who she entrusted with all the financial decisions in her life. She thought her wealth was in good hands. She'd married a financial advisor and a stock broker. He must know about money, right?

Alas, Barbara's husband was also a compulsive gambler. He ended up gambling away all her wealth that he could touch, and she divorced him, becoming a single mom with three daughters. Perhaps even worse, he moved to Israel and left her alone with a $1 million tax bill she had no idea how to pay.

When she went to ask her father to give her the money to get out of this terrible bind, he said no.

She had no choice. She had to get educated about money or she would end up on the street with her three daughters! She slowly did learn, but not without major losses first. Before fully getting educated she trusted people and invested in 2 deals that were in her words "stunning and phenomenal losses."

Barbara realized that she needed to get educated so that she would never be in that position again. During that learning process, she realized that she was called to teach others this vital lesson. As so often happens, Barbara realized that what she most needed to learn, she also most needed to help others learn as well. Thus began her journey of teaching other women about money and investing.

In the end, Barbara did get educated. She found $1 million dollars she needed to pay the tax bill, and she's made millions of dollars since teaching other women about money and wisely investing her dollars.

Lesson Learned from Barbara:

Education is a crucial part of a Real Estate Investor Goddess' Success Framework, and you may be called to share your most important lessons with the Goddess community and the world.

You can check out our incredible interview and interviews with some of the other women featured in this book at **www.RealEstateInvestorGoddesses.com**

Education helps you spot money–making opportunities

Without the proper education you can miss out on opportunities that are right in front of you.

Thus far in my investing career, I have never encountered a "losing" investment where I lost money or made a bad choice that couldn't be countered for a positive outcome. (Thank goodness, and knock on wood!) However, the more I learn about real estate, the more I smack my forehead because I realize all the opportunities I missed to invest and really grow my wealth.

For a while my husband and I were flipping houses in Los Angeles. That was fairly lucrative, but now we realize that we could have used that same money in syndications and done A LOT less work and would probably have more money to show for our efforts now. Alas, at the time we were unaware of the power of leveraging OPM - other people's money.

On the bright side, however: we know now, and when you know better, you do better. So, getting educated about real estate, its benefits, and the different asset classes are CRITICAL to being a successful investor.

Different Ways of Investing in Real Estate

The following is a brief description of some of the different ways that goddesses can invest in real estate and the different asset classes. This is NOT an all-inclusive list (there may be hundreds more ways of investing in real estate), but this includes the most common investing strategies.

As you read the description of each one, think about what sounds good or doesn't sound good about each of them. This will become useful as we help you figure out the perfect investing plan for you in the next chapter.

Strategy #1: Fix & Flip

Fix-and-flip, also called "flipping" or sometimes "rehabbing," involves buying a property that needs renovating in some form or fashion (it may need repairs, basic upkeep, or a partial or full renovation), holding it for a short term while you fix it up, and then re-selling it. The positive side of that is, if done right, you can make a quick profit. It can also be really fun to improve a property, taking an ugly duckling and make it beautiful and functional for the next seller. Lastly, it's great because the neighborhood values improve for everyone as you fix up the houses.

On the down side, flipping is more of a short-term job than an investment. When the sale is done, that's it. You have to start over again to continue to profit from this. Also, while you are holding the property you are not making money - you still have to pay mortgage, property taxes, insurance and utilities, while it's empty. You also have to pay all the rehab costs.

To flip properties successfully, it is vitally important that you have a good construction crew that's fast, affordable and does good work. When you are flipping, time is money - the longer you hold on to the property, the less money you will make at the end.

One final, very important note: That is because usually flips take less than a year to complete, and if you buy and sell the same piece of real estate within the span of a year, you won't get to take advantage of all those lovely tax benefits we discussed in Chapter 2.

Strategy #2: Buy & Hold

Buy-and-hold is exactly what it sounds like: buy the property, rent it out, and hold it long-term for cash flow. In the residential space there are three types of properties you can buy and hold:

Single Family Rentals (SFRs)

SFRs are residential homes that are rented out to one tenant, family, or set of roommates. The positive side of single-family homes is that they are relatively simple investments and often renters of single family homes may be more affluent and take better care of the home than renters in multi-family units.

The downsides of SFRs are that if the rental is empty, the property immediately has negative cash flow (no income, but you still have to pay for mortgage, property tax, and utilities), and often they are too small to justify the expense of professional property management (in other words, you are the one that gets called when the toilet backs up at 3 am).

Multifamily Units (2-4)

Multifamily residences with two to four units in the building are called duplexes, triplexes, or quad/fourplexes. Each unit in the building is rented out to a separate tenant who has their own lease. Generally, the financing for such a property is the same as for a single-family rental insofar as you can purchase these properties with residential loans. A residential loan is simpler and easier to understand for most investors – at least at first – than commercial financing (for buildings with five or more units and all other types of real estate). We will discuss the finer points of financing in Chapter 10.

The positives in a duplex, triplex, or quadplex are that when one unit is empty, you can still continue to cash flow. This gives you some leverage and economies of scale. Depending on the cash flow and the size of the property, you may also be able to afford professional property management. In other words, someone *other than you* gets the call at 3 am for that clogged toilet.

Can you tell that I don't like receiving middle of the night calls about toilets? Most of our properties are professionally managed, but we have one property that we are managing ourselves.

It's a duplex here in Los Angeles and in the interests of full disclosure, in the 12-years I've owned it, I've only received late night calls two times. We have carefully screened our tenants and have had great tenants who are super respectful of our properties, pay on time, and have lived and stayed with us for many years. For the most part, there is very little we need to do for this property and most months my only work is to cash rent checks.

Apartment Buildings/Multifamily Housing (5+ units)

Apartment buildings/multifamily housing (5+) can be used to describe anything that has 5 or more units. At this point, the major difference between a smaller multifamily residence and an apartment building other than sheer square footage is the financing. Buildings with more than five units require a commercial loan because the bank looks at this type of investment more like the purchase of a business, and in many ways it is. You are purchasing an apartment rental business.

The positive side of this investment is that you have much more leverage in terms of both time and money. Depending on the size of the building, when you have one unit empty, you may still be at 90-percent occupancy or even higher. When you make improvements and raise the rents, that also leverages very quickly both due to the increased income received and because the value of this type of property is based on Net Operating Income (NOI).

For example, if you improve a single-family home and are able to raise the rent by $50/month, you have an extra $600 of income. If you improve a 100-unit apartment building and are able to raise the rents by $50/month, that's an extra $60,000 of income. Because of the way commercial buildings are valued, in a market where the cap rates[8] are 7 percent, that $60,000 is worth an extra $857,000+ of equity.

Specialty Housing/Niche Housing
Specialty housing, or niche housing, is also pretty much exactly what it sounds like: housing with something unusual about it. In most cases, the difference will lie in your tenant population. What differentiates specialty housing is not the type of housing, (it may be single family, multi-family or an apartment building, but rather the type of tenant. These niche properties with unusual tenants may garner rental rates substantially higher than market rents.

There are three main types of specialty housing, although others may fall in and out of this category depending on the tenant in place.

Student Housing
Student housing developments are buildings around colleges and universities tailored to students. Students will often pay more for housing than other types of tenants because (a) they want to be in close proximity to a school without being in a dorm (student housing tends to be cheaper than a dorm, but more expensive than a traditional apartment), (b) they typically don't have a job or sufficient credit history to be approved for a typical apartment, and (c) students have a reputation for creating more wear and

---

[8] "Cap rate" or "Capitalization Rate" is determined by the purchase price *trends* for a comparable building in the market. It's the average rate of return on investment in that market. You can learn more about cap rates and what that means in Chapter 9.

tear on their living quarters than other renters. (Imagine renting to the fraternity brothers from the movie *Animal House!*)

Also, landlords can generally receive more rent because in student housing the lease tends to be per bed rather than per apartment, and, as in a dorm, there may even be more than one bed in a bedroom.

Here is a fairly typical example: A 3-bedroom student housing apartment with two beds per room (with each student paying $500/month) will rent for $3000/month, in a market where that similar 3-bedroom to a conventional tenant may be a $1000 - $1200/month rental.

Students may do more damage to units than typical tenants, but good property management may mitigate this. Also, each student has his/her own lease, so if one tenant has issues/ graduates, etc., it won't affect the lease for the other students in the unit.

Assisted Living Facilities

Assisted Living Facilities (ALFs) are typically single family homes that house seniors needing extra assistance with daily living. Seniors rent out bedrooms or sometimes share bedrooms in these homes, and will get assistance with daily activities like bathing and cooking.

These homes require licensing from the cities and states where they are located, and depending on the location these homes may have anywhere from six to 16 residents.

The average national rent per senior for one of these homes is $3600/month. If there are ten residents living in the home, you can see how the math adds up quickly.

The downside is that ALFs require specific trained management, and caregivers must be hired (and monitored once hired) to help the seniors with their daily tasks.

If you like the sound of owning an ALF but have concerns about your ability to manage it, you'll be happy to learn that it is possible to own the house and lease the building to an Assisted Living Facility operator. These ALF businesses will often pay 3 times the normal rent for such a home, have a long-term lease (often 5+ years), with generally much less wear and tear.

Vacation Rentals

Vacation rentals are located in areas where tourists want to come and stay and are available for short-term rental on sites like AirBnB or VRBO. Depending on how much occupancy you can get a month, these vacation rentals may bring in substantially more income per month than a typical rental.

The downside to vacation rentals is that they require more property management than a typical rental. Whenever a renter moves out (whether after one night or a couple weeks), the homes need to be cleaned, keys need to be exchanged, etc. In fact, all the things that you probably do almost habitually when you check out of a vacation location, be it a hotel or a vacation rental, will have to be handled for your vacation rental by you. There are firms that professionally manage vacation rentals, so you can hire that service out, of course. If the rents are high enough, you may be able to justify avoiding those logistical issues in person. As always, it all depends on the numbers.

Other Asset Classes

Mobile Home Parks

The term "mobile home" is a bit of misnomer. In fact, mobile homes are barely mobile at all. They are manufactured housing units built in a factory and transported to a particular plot of land. It can cost upwards of $5,000 to move one, so once the home is set down it's pretty hard to up and move it to another location.

Can it be done? Yes. Is it easy to do and, by extension, are your tenants likely to move their home right off your land? No.

A mobile home park (MHP) is a community of mobile homes. A MHP owner owns the land where the mobile homes are situated. The mobile home owner owns the home itself and pays a lot fee to the MHP to be able to stay on the land.

The big positive in MHP ownership is that the park owns the land and possibly some facilities on the land (office, laundry, etc.) but generally the MHP tenants just pay a lot fee and own their own homes.[9] If there's a toilet issue in the home, that is the homeowner's responsibility. (Yes, we are back to toilets. Can you tell, I don't like dealing with other people's bathroom facilities? Since that probably is not going to be the thing you love about real estate either, it is important to understand how you will be interacting personally with your investments and tenants, when you are making decisions about your real estate strategies.)

Another MHP positive lies in the fact that the homes are not very mobile at all. As a result, an MHP provides a very stable rental base. Once a tenant has moved his home to a mobile home park, it will not be very easy for him to up and leave. Most mobile home parks tend to be very low-rent housing options and many of the residents who live in them will have a very challenging time being able to come up with $5000 to move. Thus, mobile home park residents tend to stay a very, very long time — usually more than ten years. They also tend to have more pride of ownership because they own their homes, which is good for your property values and the level of maintenance you may be required to provide on a regular basis.

The downside is that mobile home parks tend to be very low-income housing and these parks often have the same problems associated with the lowest income areas of any town: crime,

---

[9] Some Mobile Home Parks may own some or all of the mobile homes in the park. In those cases, the mobile homes will be leased to tenants (similar to renting out a single family home or an apartment). This situation may bring in extra income, but will require more property management.

drugs, and inability to pay even the lowest rents. The parks may end up requiring very intensive management. However, as in all property investment, the better the management, the better the results.

Hospitality/Resorts/Hotels

Resorts or hotels are, in essence, very short term rentals - patrons may rent for as little as one night and upwards of a week. Depending on the location of the resort/hotel, rentals in this sector may be very seasonal.

There are different sectors in the larger hospitality sector:

- **Deluxe:** Four Seasons, Wyndham Luxury Resorts, Ritz Carlton

- **Luxury:** Sheraton, Omni, Hilton, Westin

- **Upscale:** Doubletree, Embassy Suite, Crowne Plaza

- **Boutique:** more intimate in size and scale than luxury or upscale options that strives to be one of a kind. Some examples are the Crawford Hotel in Denver, Hotel 48 Lex in Manhattan, and the Scarlet Huntington in San Francisco.

- **Midscale:** Holiday Inn, Best Western, Comfort Suites

- **Economy:** Rodeway Inn, Econo Lodge, Motel 6

- **Extended Stay:** Summerfield, Homewood Suites, Extended Stay America

The hospitality industry is tied very closely to national or even worldwide economic conditions. More prosperous times mean more travel and higher occupancy rate. In a weak economy, there is less travel. If you wish to invest in this industry, you must not only monitor current market conditions carefully, but also do your "homework" about future market cycles in order to be prepared for economic downswings.

Each of these sectors have different cycles and investment ramifications. Luxury and upscale hotels tended to be more resilient in the aftermath of the last recession, probably because they primarily cater to business travelers. However, every market is different, so investing in a high-end hotel is not a guarantee against low returns during economic downturns, although it may be a hedge or serve to "slow the bleeding" if your other investments are more susceptible.

Due to the fact that hotels require a large-scale capital investment to build and a long-term investment horizon, the industry can be slow to respond to supply and demand. When demand is high and supply is low, this may be a good investment. The downside of the lodging industry is that it is more susceptible to fluctuations in the general economy than other types of real estate.

Commercial Property (Triple Net Lease)

Commercial real estate investments involve owning a building or interest in a building that is leased to a business. The business may be a restaurant, a doctor's office, a hardware store, or anything in between.

Tenants in these properties generally have a triple net lease, also referred to in shorthand as an NNN. Triple net leases mean that in addition to rents, tenants also pay all real estate taxes, insurance, and maintenance.

A big positive in commercial investing is that you are, to a degree, "guaranteed" income with virtually no management responsibilities, long term leases, quality tenants, and stable cash flow because your tenants are responsible for nearly everything and tend to stay in place once they have moved in.

The downside is that the returns tend to be lower than in more hands-on, management-heavy investments. Also, if you lose a tenant for any reason, economy-related or otherwise, it may be harder to find a replacement (it depends on the market).

For example, you may have a dentist in your building with a 10-year lease. When the lease is up and the tenant moves out, it may take several months and sometimes even upwards of a year to find a replacement tenant since that dentist may have customized the space for dentistry or the market may simply have changed to the degree that your space is not presently in high demand.

Strategy #3: Development (New Construction)

You are considered to be investing in development or new construction if you are investing in any of the following types of properties or developments:

- You are building a property "to suit" on vacant land you purchased

- You are developing land in order to sell a building for which you believe the market has a need

- You are developing land in order to lease out the physical structures and hold the property long-term

Any commercial or residential property may be the end goal of a development/new construction investment, so this category encompasses everything from residential neighborhoods to mixed-use communities to retail spaces and office buildings.

New construction can take years to build, so the big downside is that there typically won't be a penny of profit until it's sold or rented out. Due to this increased risk (and lack of cash flow during the development period), there will likely be much more upside potential. As with any extended investment, however, it will be vitally important for you to insure that you have the time to wait on your payout and that the investment you select has a high likelihood of success based on market conditions *and management* of the project.

Strategy #4: Hard Money Lending

Some people make money in real estate by lending out their money to others to purchase properties. In hard money lending, you offer a high-interest, short-term loan to borrower so that they can secure a property. You have, in essence, become the bank.

Why offer hard money? The big attraction for many lenders is that the borrower will do the work while the lender has put their money to work at a much higher interest rate than it would at a bank or in many other investments.

Why use hard money? Investors will use hard money lenders because they have easier lending standards than a bank and will lend for shorter periods of time.

When my husband and I were flipping houses, we used a hard money lender to purchase a property. This particular property was more than we could afford with our own capital, and though we had a lot of cash in the bank at the time, we were not W2 employees and our 1040 income was low. Although we had enough money to buy the entire house outright in cash, a bank would not give us a mortgage.

We turned to a hard-money lender and got a far better deal for ourselves than we could at the bank. We got a hard money lender to give us 90 percent of the purchase price. We paid the 10-percent downpayment and the rehab costs ourselves. The interest we paid was 8.99 percent plus origination fees. This was much more than we would have paid for a mortgage from a conventional bank (at the time it would have been around 4 percent), but we couldn't get a conventional loan and we only needed the loan for approximately 6 months (time from original purchase to sale to subsequent buyer).

The good thing for us, as hard-money borrowers in this case, was that we were able to profit and we didn't have to leverage all our own money. The good thing for the hard-money lender was that this business was able to make a nice amount of cash without having to do much work. That's just another real estate investing win-win.

Strategy #5: Offshore Investing

In this book, we are going to focus primarily on investing in the United States, but there's a whole world out there, literally, that is ripe for investing. There are many options for real estate investing outside of the country - any of the above types of investments may be found and purchased offshore as well as within the United States

Why would someone want to invest offshore? There are many reasons. As with all real estate investments, you have to decide what is right for you as well as identify what is a good deal for your money.

Benefits to Offshore Investing

Here are a few reasons an investor might opt to buy real estate offshore:

Portfolio Diversification: It's always a good idea not to put all your eggs in one basket. Getting your "eggs" into international baskets can really help diversify your portfolio. If the U.S. market crashes, you may be protected by having your money/property in other markets.

Furthermore, foreign real estate has the potential for capital appreciation as well as the ability to generate cash-flows in a foreign currency from rental income. Having money in a different currency also helps with diversification.

Move Savings/Wealth Abroad: Owning foreign real estate moves your savings and wealth offshore and therefore outside of the immediate reach of your home government. Unlike with an intangible financial account (currency or paper accounts), it would be hard for your foreign real estate to be seized at the drop of a hat by your home country, without a literal act of war. It never hurts to keep at least part of your portfolio "untouchable" to the greatest extent possible!

Could Provide You With Other Residency/Citizenship: Obtaining real estate in a foreign country often provides you with some sort of residency and sometimes a shortened path to citizenship. This could provide you with a coveted second passport and visa-free travel to other countries.

Owning foreign real estate can also provide you with a second home, potentially a place to retire, and an emergency "bolt-hole" that you could, in an instant, always escape to in case of trouble in your home country.

Tax Benefits: Certain countries have very favorable tax rates compared to the U.S. Additionally, certain expenses related to searching for, purchasing, and maintaining foreign real estate are tax deductible by Americans. Consult your tax professional about other potential tax benefits.

Fund your lifestyle: Many people invest abroad because it allows them to legitimately have a business trip as a vacation. I know quite a few resort investors in Belize who do just that. They make a nice return on their investment, and get to have tax deductible trips to check on their investment.

Another example is closer to home. My parents own a home in Spain. In 2000, they decided to retire there. When their grandbabies started to be born in the United States they wanted to spend most of their time in the US and visit Spain for 3-6 months a year. Now, they have a place in Spain and a place in Los Angeles. When they are in one country, they use the other home as an Airbnb rental. In this way, their properties help pay for themselves and fund their international lifestyle.

Participate in New Markets: Not all markets are good markets and not all markets are good all the time. Markets go in cycles. At certain times in a cycle, it's a good time to buy. At other times in the cycle, it's a good time to sell. We will discuss how to find a good market in Chapter 8, but the point to remember here is that outside of the United States there may be great markets to tap into that are at the perfect point in the cycle to buy.

Downsides to Offshore Investing

Of course, there are downsides to investing in foreign real estate just as there are to any type of investing. However, offshore downsides may be a bit more complicated than those associated with investing in the United States. Things that may be a hassle for you include:

* the amount of paperwork usually required

* illiquidity of your assets

* carrying costs

* country/market specific risks

However, when those risks are weighed against the benefits, for many people owning foreign real estate is one of the best ways to diversify financial and political risk.

Strategy #6: Wholesaling

Wholesalers, sometimes referred to as "wholesellers" get a property under contract and then sell or flip the contract (taking a fee), to the ultimate buyer before closing.

Real estate investors can wholesale any type of property. I am acquainted with people who do that with single family homes, apartment buildings, mobile home parks, and commercial spaces.

The biggest benefit of wholesaling is the ability to get some money very quickly without ever having to take possession of a property, manage it, etc. The downside is that if the wholesaler doesn't find a subsequent buyer, she may end up with a property she doesn't want or need or lose her earnest money.

Strategy #7: Turnkey Investing

Turnkey investments are investments that are done completely for you. They may also be referred to as "A-to-Z" investments.

An example of a turn-key investment is single-family home that has already been remodeled, tenanted, and provided with property management. In this type of investment, you'd work with a turnkey investment operator to purchase a home. They'll help you get the mortgage and provide everything for you. You will own and receive the tax benefits and cash flow, and the work is otherwise all done for you.

The benefits of this are that there is virtually no management and everything is done for you. The downside is that as a result, returns may be lower for this type of investment.

Furthermore, you forfeit some of your control over your investment in this scenario and become nearly entirely reliant on the strength and expertise of the turn-key investment company. If they do a good job and stay around, it can be a great investment. If they aren't good property managers and your turn-key investment is outside of your market, you could be in for quite a scramble if your property manager quits or falls down on the job. In fact, you may not even know that they have failed you for weeks or even months.

As with all investments, do thorough due diligence on any companies you work with, the market, and the properties.

Strategy #8: Syndications

A real estate syndication is a group of investors that come together to purchase a property. There are two ways of investing in a syndication: actively or passively.

Actively Investing in a Syndication

Active Investors in a Syndication, also known as syndication sponsors, are involved in locating the property and bringing the other investors in to purchase.

As an active investor, you can leverage other people's money (OPM) to buy a property that is much more than you could perhaps afford by yourself. You are also diversifying the risk and opening yourself to a potentially much larger reward.

Another benefit is that in exchange for the time and energy placed into syndicating and managing the deal, active investors can receive acquisition fees, promote fees, management fees, cash flow, and/or equity.

Active investors set up a vehicle that benefits tenants, other investors, and other team members. It's very win-win. This is something that I personally do and I love it, but it's not for everyone. There are downsides.

One downside is that this is not very passive income. An active investor needs to find the property, find the investors, manage the asset or manage the property managers, and manage the syndication.

For example, as I'm writing this, we are in tax time. This week we are coordinating our bookkeeper, CPA, and property managers to make sure that all our investors have their K-1s and our various entities' tax returns are in order (each building is purchased in its own LLC). At the same time we are managing extensive rehabs on two of our buildings. Our property managers are doing the day to day management of this, but I am traveling once or twice a month to the market to make sure that things are proceeding according to plan.

But wait, there's more: we have just had a fire in one of our units. Sure, the property managers are handling the day-to-day of this, but it is our (sometimes time-consuming) responsibility to make sure that insurance and rehab are properly handled.

Lastly, we have to stay on top of our property managers to make sure they're doing a good job. We have already made several staffing changes on a property we have held for only six months. Having the right person on the job makes you money. Having the wrong person will cost you (and your co-investors), and allowing that responsibility to slide can cost you everything.

This is all to say that being an active syndicator (especially in a property that needs repositioning) can be a lot of work. After these buildings become more stable, there will be less activity on our parts and we can reduce our time spent to just a couple hours per week.

The other downside is that a sponsor may need to front a lot of the cash and time up front. This allocation of resources may not always pay off.

Passively Investing in a Syndication

A passive investor is someone who invests in a syndication, but does not have any management responsibilities on a property.

I also passively invest in properties. There are many benefits to doing so, including:

* As a passive investor, you can leverage OPM and OPT (other people's's time) to invest in a property that is much more than you afford or manage by yourself.

* Truly passive cash flow. All you have to do is pay into the deal and then wait for the checks.

There are a few downsides, however. One is that the passive investor has no control over the management of the property. You have to trust the active syndicators to do a good job to manage the property to the utmost benefit for everyone involved.

The other downside, for some, is that passive investors need to have the money to invest. Most syndicates require a hefty buy-in. Many of these syndications will require minimums of $25,000,

$50,000, or much, much more. While you may not have this money sitting around in your checking account, you still may be able to participate passively in a syndication with money you have not even considered using for real estate before today. Many people are able to passively invest with funds from their retirement accounts. You can learn more about investing in this way in Chapter 10 - Financing Your Investment.

*****

So that was an extensive, but nowhere near exhaustive list of the types of assets and ways to invest in real estate.

If you want to invest using any of the strategies I discussed, it's crucial that you further your education. You're already here and reading this book, so I'm probably preaching to the choir about the benefits of education.

I can only share so much in this book though. I encourage you to continue your education with more books, doing online courses, attending live conferences, receiving mentorship and coaching, and much more.

At Real Estate Investor Goddesses we have many resources to help you with your continuing education. Please check us out at **www.RealEstateInvestorGoddesses.com**

We provide a podcast, blog, an online membership filled with a wealth of information, coaching and mentorship, and live events. We also have a Facebook page with a great community of Goddesses to support you.

Do not invest poorly and/or miss out on the many investment opportunities right under your nose because you failed to get the education you need. We are here to support you.

Chapter Six – Your Right Vision & Plan

"Everybody that's successful lays a blueprint out."
~Kevin Hart, comedian and actor

Once you have your educational process underway, the next step is to create a personalized plan or blue print for your real estate investing. This plan should represent the combination of your unique skills, resources and desires.

The first thing to do is to ask yourself a series of questions to figure out your desires.

What are your general life goals, dreams, desires, and aspirations?

Many "coaches" in real estate will tell you to get very specific about your goals, but before you do that you have to have a clear idea about how your overall life will be affected by your successful real estate investing. So start out thinking big and broad! How do you want your life to be in general? Don't just think about real estate — think about your dreams for your life in every facet:

- career
- finances

- health

- spirituality

- family

- romance

- adventure/fun

- learning/growth

- service to others

Don't be afraid to ask yourself these questions, and then answer honestly:

- Who do you want to be with?

- What impact do you want to have on the world around you?

- How do you want to spend your leisure time?

- What work do you want to be doing?

Allow yourself to just write and fill in the following blanks in detail (use extra pieces of paper as you need or write your answers in a journal):

It is one year in the future and I am:

_____

_____

_____

_____

_____

_____

_____

_____

_____

_____

_____

_____

_____

_____

It is five years in the future, and I am:

_____

_____

_____

_____

_____

_____

_____

_____

_____

_____

_____

_____

_____

It is 20 years in the future, and I am:

_____

_____

_____

_____

_____

_____

_____

_____

_____

_____

_____

_____

_____

_____

Now that you have committed your vision and your honest desires to paper, it's time to take action and make some important decisions.

What & how do you want to invest in real estate?

Ask yourself: what do you love to do? What turns you on about real estate investing?

For me, the attraction lies in finding the properties (I really love deal hunting). I also love finding an ugly duckling and making it into something beautiful. I can look at a building and see its potential. I love reimagining it. I love the process of design and how to be strategic to create something very beautiful and luxurious for the smallest possible investment. I love the creativity of that process.

I love improving communities and making a living situation better for tenants. I love thinking creatively about how to add value for them.

I also love how "win-win" (or even win-win-win) this industry can be. I love that the sellers can get what they need and want, we and our investors can profit, and our tenants' lives are improved. I love the ripple effect of prosperity that happens on our deals and in our communities as our staff (property managers and maintenance guys), brokers, lenders, attorneys, CPAs, property managers, contractors, vendors, and more are enriched through the process.

I love syndicating and finding investors to partner with on getting these deals. I love finding out how I can serve them to reach their investment goals and create win-wins there.

I love all of this about real estate! What do you love? What *will* you love?

Maybe for you, it's just that you love the idea of getting money while you sleep. You might be thinking, "I don't want to do any of of that other stuff!" Well, that's fine! You can invest that way too. What's important is to tune into what *you* want.

So answer the question, right here and right now: what turns you on about real estate investing?

_____

_____

_____

_____

_____

_____

_____

_____

_____

_____

_____

_____

_____

_____

Now that we've established what we love about real estate investing as a concept and an industry, let's figure out how you're going to make this happen for *you*.

In the previous chapter I wrote about many different ways of investing in real estate.

Write down the 3-5 different strategies of investing in real estate/asset classes that seemed most interesting to you.

_____

_____

_____

_____

_____

_____

_____

_____

_____

_____

Now, for each one, write down WHY you like it. What turns you on about it?

_____

_____

_____

_____

_____

_____

_____

_____

_____

_____

What Resources Do You Currently Have At Your Disposal for Real Estate Investing?

Once you achieve clarity about what you want to do, it's time to get started on how you are going to do it. That's right: it's time to tally up your resources.

You need 4 main resources to invest in real estate. These resources are:

1. Money

2. Time

3. Experience

4. Relationships

We are going to help you figure out how much of these resources you currently have at your disposal. In subsequent chapters, we will help you figure out how to access any resources you might be missing.

As Tony Robbins says, **"There are no lack of resources, just lack of resourcefulness."** We will give you some ideas on how to be more resourceful.

Money – What Financial Resources Do You Have Available To You?

To buy investment property, you're going to need money. So the first thing you want to do is figure out how much money you have.

The best way to do that is to create a net worth statement. A net worth statement is a statement of your **assets** and **liabilities**.

Assets are real properties, vehicles, cash accounts, investment accounts, retirement accounts, collectable items, etc.

Liabilities include home loans, car loans, student loans, credit cards, etc.

You add up the value of your assets, subtract the total of your liabilities and the difference is your net worth.

ASSETS - LIABILITIES = NET WORTH.

You can access a worksheet to do your own net worth statement on The Real Estate Investor Goddesses website. Go to **www.RealEstateInvestorGoddesses.com** to access this.

Use this worksheet to figure out your net worth. You can also set up electronic means for maintaining your net worth statements.

I recommend Quicken (software program) or Mint (online program) for maintaining your financial net worth statement. There are many other programs that may work for you too.

To use the programs, you'll enter all your account info these programs. Your balances will be automatically updated and your net worth generated automatically.

Time - How much available time do you have for real estate investing?

When you're investing in real estate, you need:

- time to get educated/do due diligence

- time to find the property/opportunity

- time to find your team

- time to find the financing

- time to renovate the property

- time to manage the property

- time to manage other investors

As you probably noticed when you read the different way to invest in properties, there are ways to invest where you can leverage other people's time to do some or virtually all of the above. So even if you have very little time, you can still invest in real estate.

The only time you must absolutely, without question, set aside is the time to get educated about investing in general, a particular investment opportunity, and the people you may be investing with.

Do an accounting to figure out how much time you currently have at your disposal:

- Maybe you have plenty of time, but you don't have money.

- Sometimes, if you have more time than money, you can partner your time with others' money to invest.

How much time could you devote per week to your real estate investments? How is that time broken up? Can you spend a little bit of time per day? Or would you only be able to spend time in one or two bigger chunks per weeks? All of these things are important to figure out in advance since the time you are willing and able to spend will determine the scope of your real estate investing options.

_____

_____

_____

_____

_____

_____

_____

_____

_____

_____

_____

_____

_____

Now answer honestly. How do you WANT to be spending your time? Which of the above tasks seem the most fun to you? Which seem the least enjoyable? The way you feel about real estate investing *will* affect your level of success, so make sure that what you decide to do is something into which you can invest *yourself* as well as your time.

_____

_____

_____

_____

_____

_____

_____

_____

_____

_____

_____

_____

Experience - How Much Experience Do You Have in the Various Aspects of Real Estate Investment?

How much experience do you have in any of the below? Note — this experience may come from other arenas outside of real estate.

- locating a property and assessing the deal (underwriting)

- acquiring financing and/or investors

- development/renovation/managing construction or doing the work yourself

- property management (leasing/dealing with tenants)

- project management

- book keeping/accounting/taxes

Assess and then answer honestly.

_____

_____

_____

_____

_____

_____

_____

_____

_____

_____

_____

_____

_____

_____

_____

Relationships – To Whom Are You Connected Who Could Help You Acquire and Manage Your Investments?

If you find that you're lacking in any other resource (money, time, or experience), you can bridge the gap through relationships. You can partner with others to:

- find deals

- find financing

- manage the asset (tenants/construction etc.)

Who do you know who has experience in any of the areas we talked about above? If you don't know someone personally, who do you know who *might* know someone? Use the space below to create a list of resources and references.

_____

_____

_____

_____

_____

_____

_____

_____

_____

_____

_____

_____

_____

Real Estate is all about relationships. It is a team sport. The stronger your team, the better your outcomes. In the next chapter, we will talk about who you need on your winning real estate investment team, and how to create that team.

Chapter Seven – Your Right Team

"Teamwork makes the dream work, but a vision becomes a nightmare when the leader has a big dream and a bad team."
~ John C. Maxwell, Author, Speaker & Business Visionary

"Work with the best. The best will make you money. The worst will lose you money."
~Beth Clifford, Boutique International Developer

The foundation of any good real estate investment is a great team. A great team will help you to find the right property, get the financing, protect the assets, and manage the assets when you have them. A bad team, on the other hand, could turn a great potential investment into a complete loss.

In this chapter, we are going to share with you some of the most important people you will need to have on your team and three steps to assembling the best team.

Who do you need on your team?

Broker/Agent

A real estate broker or real estate agent will help you find, buy, and/or sell your property (at the appropriate time, of course). You want to choose an experienced broker/agent who *really knows your asset class.*

If you are purchasing any residential real estate with 5 or more units, commercial, industrial, etc., work with an experienced commercial real estate broker. These types of deals are very different from residential (1-4 units)[10] and you want someone who can navigate this space with confidence, insight, and experience.

A good experienced broker/agent will be invaluable to you. They will:

- guide you to properties (even some that are off-market (e.g., they have not officially been put on the market for sale),

- know the market well,

- help you to find the right deal for you, and

- have referrals for the rest of the team.

Property Manager

A professional property manager will manage your property once you take ownership. Your property manager(s) will:

- collect rents

- provide/arrange for repair & maintenance services (they handle those broken toilets!)

- collect and maintain security deposits

- lease out vacant units

- provide accounting services - handle accounts and pay the bills

- inspect properties

---

[10] See Chapter 9 on Choosing the Right Property, on some of the differences between residential and commercial properties.

- handle evictions if necessary

Good property management is invaluable.

A good property manager will help attract and keep great tenants. They will keep things running optimally with little input from you so all you need to do is collect checks.

Bad property management, on the other hand, can quickly sink your property's income and value. A property manager who chooses to lease to bad tenants who don't pay and/or vandalize a property, or who causes good tenants to leave because the manager is rude or doesn't handle maintenance issues promptly, can take down your smoothly-running investment ship in no time – often before you are even aware there is a problem! Another property manager flaw to look for: a manager that is not paying bills on time and/or antagonizing your vendors.

How your property is managed will make or break your investment. Make sure you work with the best property manager possible.

A great property manager is also helpful BEFORE you purchase because they know the market very well and can help steer you in the direction of good deals and/or steer you from bad deals. A property manager can also help you work out a budget to ensure you have sufficient funds, and connect you to other members of the team.

Lender

You might not think of your lender as being your partner, but they are. The lender gives you a loan to purchase the property. They will likely be the biggest investor in terms of interest in the property!

A lender will make sure that you have enough money to be successful. For a residential loan (1-4 units), the lender will look at your credit score and income (including 75 percent of the rental income from the property) to assess your ability to take on the loan.

A commercial lender will make sure that you have a winning business plan and have enough money to be successful; if the deal is good enough they will sometimes help you find the right partners too to make it happen.

Attorney

Alas, we live in a a litigious society. One way to protect yourself, your real estate portfolio, and any investors you may have, is to purchase each of your properties using a business entity (typically Limited Liability Corporations - LLCs). An attorney can help you set up the business entities to do this and advise you on the best way to structure these businesses in your unique situation.

If you are buying with other individuals and investing with their money, you will definitely need to work with a securities attorney to make sure you don't violate any securities laws and structure that deal correctly. Attorneys can also help you draft and/or review contracts/leases.

Insurance Agent

You need to make sure your property is well-insured or you could lose your money *and* your property. Also, in order to get financing from a lender, you will almost certainly need to have property insurance.

If you are syndicating, you should also have Director's and Officer's (D&O) Insurance and Errors and Omissions (E&O) Insurance to protect you as well. Remember what I said above about living in a litigious society? Proper insurance will help protect you.

A good insurance agent will make sure you have the right amount of insurance (not too much and not too little) at the best price.

CPA/Accountant

Remember all those tax benefits I talked about in Chapter 2? A CPA will help you make sure your real estate business is set up structurally to take best advantage of them.

Make sure you get a CPA/Accountant that is knowledgeable about investment property; preferably one that is a real estate investor him or herself.

Contractor

Find and partner up with a great contractor before you buy. They can help you assess properties to determine how much work will be needed and how much that work will cost. No one can see through walls (there are often surprises), but an experienced contractor will be able to spot signs of bigger issues. You can use these bigger issues to either negotiate the price down or you may decide to walk away.

If you don't plan to do any work upon purchasing the property (and even if you do), also hire a Home Inspector/Property Inspector to make sure you spot any potential issues.

Lastly, if you plan to buy a property that needs some fixing up (something I recommend doing in order to get the best bang for your buck), your contractor can let you know how much your planned improvements will cost so you can make sure you get the financing you need.

Self-Directed IRA Provider

You might be wondering - "what is a Self- Directed IRA and why would I need a Self-Directed IRA Provider?" That's a question I wondered myself when I first heard about self-directed retirement accounts about 18 months ago.

A SDIRA is an individual retirement account that gives you complete control over your investment choices.

Most people have IRAs or 401k's in plans offered through their employers or through one of the bigger financial institutions – Fidelity, Ameritrade, Charles Schwab, etc. In these accounts, there is a limited set of options of what you can invest in – generally a very limited menu of mutual funds and bonds.[11]

Using a Self-Directed IRA provider, you can convert these accounts into an SDIRA that will enable you to invest in real estate (and pretty much anything else in which you might want to invest).

There is a small list of prohibited transactions (basically you can't invest in collectibles, life insurance, or things that personally benefit you and your family), but you can invest in nearly anything else.

Because you can't use your SDIRA to "personally benefit you and your family," you can't use these funds to buy a house you'd live in, but it is a perfect vehicle to buy investment property.

So if you have been wondering "how do I find any money to invest?" Well, you might be sitting on tens, or hundreds of thousands of dollars in your retirement account that could be bringing you much better returns in a much safer investment if you invest in real estate.

If you own your own business you can convert those funds not just to an SDIRA, but to a SD-401k. My husband used his SD-401k to passively invest in a 516-unit property in Atlanta.

A SD-retirement funds provider will help you convert your funds, so they are available for your use.

---

[11] I remember being very annoyed at one point because I wanted to put the bulk of my money in a low-fee S&P 500 Index fund (hey, if it's good enough for Warren Buffett...), and that option wasn't even available.

Co-Sponsors/Co-Investors

If you plan to purchase a property with other people, using your knowledge of OPM and OPT to get your start in the game, then you will need to find some investing partners.

When you are looking for a partner, you should be looking for someone with complimentary skills and resources to those that you already have. You want someone who is like-minded to you, but you don't want someone *just like you.* You are building a team, not a clone army!

Here are a few tips for finding good partners (co-investors or co-sponsors) for your team and your deals:

1. **Do proper due diligence on any partners**
   Make certain that your future partners are a good fit for you personally and that they have the skills, experience, and character traits that they claim to.

2. **Listen to your intuition**
   If that little voice inside says "Yes, this is the person!" then consider that a blessing. If it whispers "No, this is not a good fit," be willing to listen as well. Even if a person is the logical choice for you, if your intuition does not like the fit be very hesitant to move forward.[12]

   The few decisions I've ever regretted in my life are the ones I made after hearing that voice and then choosing to go in a different direction than instructed. *I have never regretted listening to my intuition, and neither will you.*

---

[12] See Chapter 11 for more information on how to hone your intuition.

3. **Have a Clear Contract in Place**

Whenever you partner with anyone, have a clear contract in place. Everyone's responsibilities and rights should be laid out so that all parties know what is expected of them and agree to perform to those expectations. A contract should also provide clear exit strategies. Whether things actually "go south" or the time simply comes to move on, the contract will protect all parties and assist in a graceful exit.

Warning: You may be tempted to think, *"This is my best friend/brother/etc. We don't need a contract! We love each other and understand exactly what we are doing!"*

The moment you get involved in business with your best friend/brother/etc. is when you need a contract most!

I've seen so many relationships fail because the parties involved were not all on the same page about what they were actually supposed to be doing. They did not, in the end, have the same goals or vision and, worse, they did not have a good way to exit the business relationship while retaining the personal one.

A good, clear contract can actually help preserve a relationship.

As my mentors, The Real Estate Guys, always say, "We seek relationships for life." A clear contract will help you establish and maintain those relationships.

Mentors

Last, but certainly not least, you need at least one mentor on your team. A good mentor will help:

- Motivate you
- Coach you
- Inspire you
- Teach you
- Guide you
- Provide a vision for you
- Lead by example

A mentor should be someone who is actually investing in real estate and who is, in some capacity, already operating in a position in which you also want to be. For example, they may have a thriving business, an incredible attitude, or great creativity in real estate. Whatever you hope to model from them, make sure they have managed to achieve that themselves.

As one of my teachers, Michael Stevenson, wrote:

> Don't take business advice from people who are failing at business. Choose mentors who are ACTUALLY doing what you want to do, making a real impact and living the lifestyle that you want to live. Just because someone has a lot of Facebook followers DOESN'T mean they know what they are talking about.

Personally, my husband and I have invested in mentorship programs with The Real Estate Guys, Brad Sumrok, and Kyle Wilson. Those relationships have proven invaluable.

At Real Estate Investor Goddesses, we offer both private and group mentoring available for women who want to invest more successfully in real estate in a way that honors the feminine. Go to **www.RealEstateInvestorGoddesses.com** to find out more.

***

Now that you have a blueprint to use as you assemble your real estate investing team, get started building that team roster!

Make sure that you choose people with whom you will enjoy working, and who you like and trust.

Within those parameters, **seek out the best, most experienced professionals available to you.** Ideally, each of your team members will be property investors themselves and will understand and appreciate the unique opportunities and challenges of property management and real estate portfolio ownership.

Working with the best WILL make you money in the end while creating the best outcomes for all involved. Keeping that win-win outcome in mind is critical to assembling a winning team.

***

Now that you know who you need on your team, how do you go about finding these team members and creating these crucial relationships you will need to success in real estate?

Start with these three steps.

The 3 steps to building strong relationships:

1. Think about the future team members you already know.

You are already connected to a lot more people than you think.

Make a list of all the people who you know that are involved in real estate. They could be service providers or investors themselves.

Surf your LinkedIn connections, contacts databases, or your Facebook friend list to jog your memory. You probably know more people than you thought you knew.

Next think about who you know that's influential - who might know of someone that could help you. Everyone you know has at least 10 contacts and sometimes hundreds or thousands of other contacts. You are likely only one or two degrees of separation from anyone you would want to meet.

2. Put yourself in situations where you'll meet the right people.

The connections my husband and I have certainly enabled the pretty extraordinary results we've accomplished.

Here's a secret: those connections did not happen by accident.

We have purposefully put ourselves in the room with people that are doing real estate (and life) at the highest levels. We have invested a lot in conferences and mentorship, and it has paid off.

As of this writing, I just got back from spending 9 days at sea with 195 incredible real estate investors on The Real Estate Guys' *Investor Summit at Sea.* It was a large investment of time and treasure, but it paid off in terms of what I've learned and the industry influencers with whom I was able to connect.

I met and shared meals with Robert Kiyosaki, author of *Rich Dad, Poor Dad.* It was unbelievable to get to know the man whose book set me on the course to being a full time real estate investor. I also met and spent time with Kenny McElroy, author of the *ABCs of Real Estate Investing,* Tommy Hopkins, sales guru and author of *How to Master the Art of Selling,* and many more.

Not everyone is able to go to as many conferences and events as I do or even wants to, but you all have the ability to get yourselves to events where you'll be able to connect with the right people to take you to the next level. Attend a local real estate investors' association (REIA) meeting, or hit a private lenders' Meetup while you're on a business trip anyway. These things are inexpensive (if not free) to attend and will help you make connections that will change your business and your life.

Furthermore, don't just attend these events and then sit in the corner! Seek to meet as many people as you can. When you meet these great people, make sure to follow up with them. And don't forget to do Step Three.

3. Show up and be of service.

You may be wondering, "*Why would someone want to work with me? I'm new or not as successful as they are.*"

The way to get the best people to work with you is not to focus on how they can help you, but to focus on how you can help them.

Look for ways to be of service and to solve their problems.

Here's the good news: it doesn't even have to be a big problem that you are solving. Just demonstrating that you are considerate and helpful, will make a huge impression. They will want to work with you if you provide an opportunity and/or can help them solve a problem.

Here's an example:

When we were just starting out in Albuquerque, we were under contract, but we needed lots of help to get the deal over the finish line. We did not have any experience at that point and we needed to raise over $2,000,000 without much of a database.

We found a great partner with more experience and a much larger investor database than us. He was happy to partner, because at that point we had two deals in hand and a great local team in place – property management company, broker, attorney, CPA, and lender.

We showed up, did the work, and found ways to be of service. Continuing to do that has opened us up to many more opportunities and contributes to our results.

Those are my three steps to creating successful relationships. Now what are you doing to set up strategic relationships in your life?

Chapter Eight – Your Right Market(s)

"Live where you want to live. Invest where the numbers make sense." ~Robert Helms, Real Estate Guys Radio Host

"The market is more important than the property." ~Ken McElroy, *The ABCs of Real Estate Investing*

The number one rule of Real Estate Investing is "Location! Location! Location!"

Whether or not your property will make money has almost everything to do with its location.

So how do you find the right market and submarket that will allow you to profit with your real estate investments? I'll show you in this chapter!

First, though, let's take a moment to talk about the *4 biggest myths that people have about property markets that keep them from profiting:*

4 Biggest Myths About Markets:

Myth #1: You have to invest where you live

Truth: You can invest wherever the numbers makes sense (and they may not make sense where you live).
This is a myth that I used to believe wholeheartedly. My husband and I live in Los Angeles, one of the most expensive markets in the U.S., and we were looking to buy a multi-unit property that we could buy and hold.

We searched and searched in and around Los Angeles but couldn't find anything that we could afford to buy, or if we could afford it would make us any money.

I got very frustrated until I met Robert Helms and he shared that quote from the beginning of the chapter with me: "Live where you want to live. Invest where the numbers make sense."

I had never before considered investing outside of where I lived and could easily drive.

Hearing him say that to me was a big paradigm shift. It literally opened up the entire world to my real estate portfolio. If we found the right market with the right numbers, we could literally invest anywhere.

Dear reader, I want you to remember this maxim too: Live where you want to live, invest where the numbers make sense.

Myth #2: You have to buy a in place that you'd want to live.

Truth: The best investment opportunities are often in areas where you wouldn't want to live.

Again, it comes down to "live where you want to live, invest where the numbers make sense." I want to live in a large 6-bedroom house overlooking the ocean in Santa Monica, CA, but I would not buy such a place as an investment property.

Buying such a property, would not make sense for my investment goals of 10 percent yearly cash-on-cash return. If I were to buy such a place and try to rent it, chances are I would not be able to rent it out for enough money to profit on it at all.

For me, I'd rather purchase in markets that have all the factors of a great market (see below) and are in a lower- to middle-income neighborhood.

These are often not in the best parts of town and may not be in the parts of town with the best schools, so I probably wouldn't choose to move my family there. However, these are areas with lots of renters and where my investment dollar will likely go the farthest.

Myth #3: Being in a good city is enough.

Truth: You need to be in the right submarket - sometimes success can be the difference of a block.

Let's start with an example: Let's say that you are considering buying rental property in Dallas, Texas. You did your homework and concluded that Dallas is the right market for you. Now, it's time to buy anything you can get your hands on, right? Stop! Wrong!

Knowing Dallas meets your investment criteria is a great start, but that alone does not mean that all the neighborhoods in Dallas are appropriate locations for you to purchase and own investment properties.

You must find the right submarket. Sometimes being on the "wrong side of the tracks" can be the difference between success and failure.

When people are deciding where to rent, they consider the same things that you probably considered before your last move: school district, crime in the area, proximity to major employers, proximity to public transportation, proximity to shops, restaurants, and other area of interest, etc. You must consider these same things in order to ultimately purchase a rental property that will attract good, reliable renters.

Just because any city "as a whole" is a good city for investors, it doesn't mean that every neighborhood within it will be a good fit for you to invest in.

Sometimes, the difference between success and failure can be even smaller than neighborhood by neighborhood. Sometimes a particular street can make the difference.

You'll want to learn the market and the submarkets well in order to make the best investment decision possible.

Myth #4: You can learn everything you need to know by researching online.

Truth: Usually it will take you getting your boots on the ground or the boots of someone you really, really, really trust on the ground before you can make an educated decision.

You can find a lot of information about a market online: population rates, new employers coming to town, population demographics, etc., but there are certain things that you will only know by visiting

When you visit a location, you will get a feel for the market and the people. You will also be able to meet with and talk to your team and drive the neighborhoods and streets. You can see a lot from Google Earth, but you might not be able to see how far that public transportation really is or that there is a homeless encampment in the alley behind the property you're interested in.

If you are not able to visit your market, you must have someone you really trust, both in terms of their integrity and their judgment, to make an educated assessment to visit for you. Sometimes your property management company can visit for you.

These properties will likely be the biggest financial investment you make in your life, so it will behoove you to see them yourself if at all possible.

Let's say it again: ***"Live where you want to live. Invest where the numbers make sense."***

So how do you find the right market with the right numbers? Here are 6 factors that you want to look out for:

The 6 Factors to Consider When Choosing a Market

1. Landlord & Business Friendly

2. Low to Median Cost of Housing

3. High Job Growth & High Population Growth

4. Familiarity

5. Appropriate Submarket

6. Buy in the Right Market Cycle

Let's take a look at these more closely one by one.

1. Landlord & Business Friendly

When you are investing in real estate, you (a) are likely going to be a landlord and (b) have a real estate business. It's best to invest in communities that are friendliest to landlords and businesses.

Let me give you an example of two markets where we have properties - Los Angeles & Dallas.

A Tale of Two Markets: Los Angeles vs. Dallas

We have a duplex that we own in Los Angeles. We are very lucky that over the years we have had great tenants that pay their rent on time. If our tenants decided to stop paying rent for whatever reason and we had to evict them it could take us upwards of six months to do that. That's how long the process can take in Los Angeles.

That means for the six months they are not paying, we still would have to pay mortgage, taxes, and sometimes utilities for them to be there. That's in addition to all the eviction costs. Also, while they're there you cannot rent it out to someone else who will pay. It's a terrible situation for a landlord to encounter, and this precise scenario has sent more than a few landlords hurtling toward bankruptcy and foreclosure.

Now, that does not necessarily mean that you should never invest in Los Angeles. There are situations that may not be so terrible for a landlord, such as when you have many units over which to spread the costs while you are evicting a non-performing tenant. If you are renting out a single-family house or a duplex or triplex, however, losing out on all that rent for half a year or more, could put you in jeopardy of losing your property!

Another way in which Los Angeles is very tenant-friendly (as opposed to landlord-friendly) is through rent control and other housing protections.

With rent control, most tenants are guaranteed the ability to stay in a rent-controlled apartment at the rent-controlled rent pretty much *forever.* That's a great idea in theory because it helps tenants remain in their homes. In practice, however, it means that as property taxes and other real estate *ownership* expenses rise, landlords' hands can be tied in terms of making enough money to handle them.

If you a buy a multi-unit property and you have tenants that are paying below market rents you can only require one tenant to leave, *and* you must pay them a very generous moving fee to do so. The other tenants will be able to stay as long as they want and rents can only be increased 3 percent per year indefinitely.

Here's an example of how rent control can end up hurting a landlord and even the tenants as well:

Let's say you want to buy a four-unit building, a quadplex. Market rents in the area are $1500 per month, but your tenants are on month-to-month leases and paying around $600 per month. You can require the occupants of one unit to vacate (though you have to pay them a $5000/person moving fee). So, let's say you move out a family of 3. You can require them to move, but you have to pay them a $15,000 moving fee. Now you can charge $1500/month for that apartment, but it will be 10 months before you've even broken even, and that does not include the carrying costs you may accrue while you are moving the tenant out of that one unit.

As for the other units, month-to-month means they can give *you* a month's notice to vacate, but you cannot force them to leave *ever*. To evict them they would have to either stop paying rent or do something else extreme to violate other provisions of their lease. Even then, it can still take upwards of six months for the eviction.

If those tenants remain, you can raise their rents only 3 percent each year. That means a year after your purchase, you can raise rent to $618, but that is nowhere near the $1500 + 3% market rent ($1545) the other unit will get. And the disparity will grow over time so you'll always be way below market rate on those units.

Unless you're practically gifted the building in the first place, it's very hard to make those numbers pan out.

Now, let's contrast Los Angeles with Dallas, Texas. In Dallas, you can evict a tenant for non-payment in 3 weeks. So, if your tenant is late on rent once, you can have them out and their place back on the market and ready to be leased in one month. From the very start, if you have a bad situation with a tenant you will be able to "stop the bleeding" nearly six times faster than you would in Los Angeles.

Also, there is no rent control in Dallas. That means if you bought a fourplex where everyone was month-to-month and paying below market rents, none of those tenants have a right to stay in your property and pay cripplingly low rents. You can give them 30 days' notice of a change in rent to market rates and/or give them a 30-day notice to vacate. They'd have to start paying the new rent or be out in 30 days.

As a landlord, can you see how that would be more attractive?

Business Friendliness:

The other thing to consider is how business-friendly a city and state are. In a 2016 CNBC poll, California was ranked 50th (least friendly) on the list of business-friendly states. Texas was ranked #1.

The things that are considered on these rankings are: business costs, labor supply, regulatory environment, economic climate, growth prospects and tax climate.

As soon as you buy an investment property, you are in the real estate business. This means you now have to consider a new set of tax issues outside of your personal obligations! So, when you're buying in a market, property and business taxes will personally be a factor, as will things such as the ease in getting permits and licensing.

You don't just want tax-friendliness, either. You want business-friendliness. These two usually go hand in hand, but it pays to evaluate them separately. Are you investing in a place that is business friendly and will bring in more businesses and jobs and, by extension, more renters for you?

As we will talk about more in section 3 below, you also want to invest in a place with high job growth. If you're in a business-friendly environment, you're more likely to be in an environment with high job growth.

2. Low to Median Cost of Housing

The next factor in a good investment property market is to have low to median cost of housing.

Cost of housing is important because (a) it will determine your ease in being able to enter the market (the more expensive a market, the harder it will be for you to purchase there), and (b) you will have to be able to charge a lot more for rent to get back your return on investment if you are renting to tenants with stable, well-paying jobs.

Let's talk about Los Angeles again.

The good thing about Los Angeles (for landlords seeking tenants, anyway) is that it's very hard for most people to buy a home, so there are many people renting. There's also a housing shortage in the city, so there are more renters than available apartments. This means rents continue to rise and the city has some of the highest rents in the nation.

The downside is that this is all factored into the cost of the buildings so that (a) buildings are extremely expensive and (b) it can be hard to charge enough rent to cover all your costs - mortgage, property taxes, and other expenses.

Let's say you are looking to buy a quadplex in a middle-class area of Los Angeles. You can easily pay upwards of $300,000 - $400,000 per unit (or $1.2 to $1.6 million for the building). Let's say you want to buy a building that's $1,400,000 ($350,000 per unit).

If you put 20 percent down ($280,000) and get a 4 percent interest rate, your monthly mortgage payment will be about $5,321 per month. Property taxes will be about $1482 per month and your home insurance will be about $257 per month. This will be a total monthly outlay of $7,060 per month.[13]

To *merely break even* each of your units need to pay $1,765/ month in rent.

If you can rent those units out for $2,000 per month (average rent for a 1-bedroom in LA), that's $940/month in profit or $11,280. The initial investment was $280,000 to purchase the building. That means your yearly return on investment is only about 4 percent. So, you do own a cash-flowing investment property in Los Angeles, but compared to other locations where you might own a similar property, your return on investment is pretty low.

Los Angeles Quadplex Breakdown

$280,000 - 20% down payment

$5321 - mortgage payment (principle plus interest - 4%)

$1482 - property taxes

$257 - homeowners insurance

$7060/month total[14]

$1765/month break even

$2000/month = 4% ROI
(average rent for a 1-bedroom in Los Angeles).

---

[13] For simplicity sake, we're not factoring in other costs, like property management, landscaping, utilities, time when units are not rented, advertising costs, make-ready costs, and other expenses that will add to the bottom line.

[14] Numbers from Redfin® Calculator

Now, let's take a look at Dallas.

Let's contrast this with a quadplex I found available in a middle class area of Dallas for $625,000

$125,000 - 20% down payment

$2390 - mortgage payment (principle plus interest)

$554 - property taxes

$568 - homeowner's insurance

$3512/month total[15]

$878/month break even

$1008/month = 5% ROI
($997/month is the average rent for a 1-bedroom in Dallas)

In Dallas, it's considerably cheaper for a real estate investor to get in the game. You can get 2 or more buildings for the same investment you made to get one building in Los Angeles.

In this example above, the returns aren't that different (though when you go bigger, the cap rates will change. In Los Angeles, the stabilized cap rate in a B Class neighborhood is currently 5.5 - 6.5. In Dallas, the stabilized cap rate in a B Class neighborhood is 8.25 - 9.[16] That means you're getting about 3 percent more on your investment in Dallas than you are in Los Angeles.

3. High Job & Population Growth

You want your investment property located in a place where people (a) want to live and (b) can afford to pay your rents.

---

[15] Numbers from Redfin® Calculator

[16] CBRE North America Cap Rate Survey First Half 2016

Where there is high job growth, there usually is population growth as well. People tend to follow jobs, and people with jobs can pay your rent.

Typically, you'll want to avoid places that have no job growth or population growth. And you definitely want to avoid places that have no jobs or population at all!

A Cautionary Tale

A few weeks ago I received an email from a woman in the Real Estate Investor Goddesses community requesting my help with some property she owns.

Back in the 1980s, she'd been convinced to invest in some land in Belen, New Mexico. This land was about 35 miles outside of Albuquerque. She'd been convinced to buy this land in the desert under the assumption that Albuquerque was going to balloon outward and this land would be soon developed. She never visited the land, but it sounded like a great deal. She paid $5000 per acre and bought 50 acres (a $250,000 investment).

At the time she bought the land, it was completely empty - no houses, no offices, not even any electricity or water hook-ups. It was certainly a speculative investment and, unfortunately, things haven't gone as she had hoped or been led to believe they would....

To make a long story short, roughly 35 years later that land has never been developed. *Well that's not that bad,* you may be thinking. *She can just sell to someone who will develop it or who wants to hold vacant land long-term.* That is, in fact, what she's hoping to do, but at this point, the potential (or lack of potential) for the land is pretty evident. In fact, she's been told she'll be lucky to get back $1,000 per acre on this land, though "maybe soon there *might* be some development..."

I'd been investing in Albuquerque, so she wanted to know if I knew anything or anyone who could help her. I put her in touch with a broker and wished her luck. In this case, however, I'm not feeling particularly optimistic that more than three decades of holding that land are going to yield the fruit she had hoped when she made the initial investment, though.

Maybe the land will be developed sometime soon and will be more valuable, but right now it's only worth 20% of what she paid for it 35 years ago.

By comparison, if that money had been invested in a CD account at a bank at 5% compound interest, today it would be worth over $1,379,000.

This is a cautionary tale of what can happen when you buy the wrong property in the wrong market, when you don't get out there and do your due diligence in person, and when you trust someone who doesn't have all the information that they purport to or who simply cannot be trusted.

So what should you do *right now*?

Start looking for a market with high job growth and high population growth TODAY.
Don't try to buy something that "may" have job and population growth sometime in the future.   If you do that, you are gambling with your money.

Search for markets that have several large employers.

We have all seen and heard the stories of once bustling cities that had one big employer. When that employer closed the one factory, the people who were employed by the factory lost their jobs, but it also negatively affected all the ancillary businesses that relied on that factory - the parts suppliers, the restaurants, the dry cleaners, and yes, the property owners that housed the workers or leased their commercial space to the businesses.

When the one big employer leaves town, it destroys the whole economy. Seek out markets with lots of employers and new ones coming in.

Look for economic diversity.
You want multiple employers, and a market with multiple industries. Sometimes entire industries can be taken down, and you want to invest in an area with an economy that can withstand this kind of blow.

For example, some coal mining areas in Appalachia may have had several different mining companies operating locally, but that was the only industry. The towns may have survived one coal company shutting down, but when the coal industry as a whole started hurting, it took the whole economy down.

I'll share later on in the chapter about how you can find information out about a market's economic drivers.

Search for areas that have "clearly defined personas."
These are unique areas of a town that have a distinct personality that people want to live in.

"Places that have clearly defined personas are population draws almost as powerful as employment"
   ~Ken McElroy (*ABCs of Real Estate Investment*)

Venice Beach in California (highest rents per capita in the whole country) is a beach city with an edgy, irreverent vibe. It's located in Los Angeles and is surrounded by beautiful beach cities, but it is distinct from even all the other beach cities around. Venice Beach does have several large employers now, but people are mostly drawn to live there because of its persona.

I considered Kansas City and Albuquerque as investment markets. I chose Albuquerque because it had more of a persona to me. Personally, it was someplace that I found more interesting and preferred to "have to visit" when I checked in on my investments.

Within Albuquerque I chose a submarket called Uptown. Uptown is a growing area near some of the biggest and trendiest shops - a series of upscale outdoor malls. It has a definite personality and cache that is more attractive than many other parts of town. Because of that, it can fetch higher rents.

4. Familiarity

Invest in markets that you and/or your team members know really well. You can get a lot of information online, but it's not the same as having an intimate familiarity with the market you're investing in.

That's why most people do invest in the market where they live. They know and understand the market. They know where the good neighborhoods are and where the bad neighborhoods are. They know where the new employers are coming in and where they're looking to go.

When you're familiar with an area and interact with the people and business entities within it, you may find out about projects or employers that are "likely" or "about to" make the move before it's public, and be able to purchase the right property in the right place.

If you're not living in the market, you must correspond regularly with lots of people who are living in the market or investing in the market. Ask their opinions on what's happening and where are the promising areas or areas to avoid.

Take a trip to the property market and set up appointments with brokers, property managers, and city officials. Ask them what they're seeing in the market, where employers are coming, where people are moving, what's the place in town that's up and coming.

An educated investor is a profitable investor. This educated familiarity with a market is crucial in making good decisions with your money in that market.

5. Targeting Appropriate Submarkets

Not all neighborhoods in a city are created equal for investment purposes. You have to find the right neighborhood/submarket to meet your investment goals.

When people are looking for where to rent they consider things like:

> -school district
>
> -crime in the area
>
> -proximity to major employers
>
> -proximity to public transportation
>
> -proximity to shops, restaurants, parks, and other area of interest, etc.

These are things you should consider too. Look very carefully at the different neighborhoods and even different areas within neighborhoods. Sometimes being on or off a particular street can make all the difference.

You'll often hear brokers and investors use terms like "Class A," "Class B," "Class C" and even "Class D" to describe neighborhoods. At this point it's helpful to define the different classes of neighborhood.

Class A

These are the "hottest," most expensive areas. They'll have trendiest restaurants, bars and shops. They'll have the wealthiest people and the highest-cost real estate.
Examples: Beverly Hills, the Upper East Side of Manhattan, South Beach Miami

Class B

This is one step down from Class A. They are slightly older areas, with still-decent restaurants and schools. This area will lack some of the finer amenities of Class A neighborhoods. These are "middle class" areas of town.

Class C

Class C neighborhoods generally have older properties (30 years of age or more). These areas will also attract people who are on government subsidies or working low-wage jobs. You might find a lot of cash-checking business, pawn shops, liquor stores, etc. in these areas.

Often people will just talk about Classes A-C, but sometimes you'll hear about Class D real estate as well.

Class D

A class D neighborhood is the type of place you probably wouldn't want to be alone, even in the daytime. These are the "war zone" areas of town. These are high-crime areas where you might find gangs and rampant drug use. In a Class D neighborhood, there may be a lot of vacant buildings with boarded up windows.

Investing in Class D is generally only for people who are very brave and really, really know what they're doing. If you're a new investor, I wouldn't recommend you investing in a Class D neighborhood.

We have an apartment in a Class C neighborhood and even that has had its shares of challenges. In six months we have already had a tenant with a drug overdose, a tenant go to jail, a drive-by shooting, and a fire that turned out to have started over a lovers' quarrel gone very wrong. These were tenants we had inherited, and at this point we are resolving the problem. We have tougher leasing standards now and *hopefully* we won't have such problems in the future, but that's what you can expect when you're working in Class C. Class D is that much worse.

Class descriptions can also be used to describe a property's designated and/or best use. We'll define those in the next chapter.

Keep in mind: You must always keep your focus on neighborhoods that are a fit for your investment needs.

6. Buying in the Right Market Cycle

There are typically four cycles in a real estate market - the upturn, boom, downturn, and stabilization.

Upturn indicates a rising market. A lot of the factors I share with you are about finding a market that's turning upward. It is growing in population and employers. People are coming in. It's still in the upswing and there are many opportunities to be found.

Boom is when a market is already HOT, HOT, HOT. Everyone knows about this market and wants to be there. It's growing, but at the top end of its growth cycle.

Downturn is when the market begins to contract. Population is declining, jobs are leaving. Avoid these at all costs.

Stabilization is when a market is holding steady. There's not a lot of growth or movement one way or the other.

The ideal location in which to invest is a market currently heading for an upturn, a "rising" market. This is generally the best way to be able to find a deal that will quickly gain in equity and give you the best returns.

If you are unable to find a rising market, then you may need to look elsewhere for something that meets your specific needs. I personally prefer to look in stable, mature markets if I do not find a rising market that suits my investment strategies when I am ready to make a real estate investment purchase.

In a stable market, there won't be much equity gain from the market itself, but there are ways to find a good building that you can "force" equity into. We will talk about that more in the next chapter.

Third down on my list of preferences, is the Boom Market. I typically avoid buying in markets that are "hot, hot, hot" because they are sellers' markets. If you're a buyer in a sellers' market, it's by definition NOT a buyer's market. In other words, it's going to be very difficult to find a good deal. If you're in the feeding frenzy, it's likely you'll just get scraps.

There ARE ways to find some decent deals in a boom market, but that generally requires you to have excellent relationships with people in the market that can help you find certain "off-market" deals. As a general rule, unless you already have these relationships, I'd avoid these markets.

Lastly, there's the down-turning market. Avoid these markets if your goal is to cashflow and make money now. If people and employers are leaving town, there won't be the necessary population to rent your properties. This is not to say that you cannot make money on a property purchased during a downturn, but you will need a long-term plan and the financial wherewithal to execute it, including potentially paying the note on the land for an indeterminate length of time while you wait for things in the area to change.

How do you find necessary market information?

Search Google for general information about the major markets in your target area.

First do macro searches on Google. You can look in the general areas you want to be. Maybe search for all the major markets within a 2- to 3-hour flight of your home.

I personally like being able to fly to my market, visit for a few hours as necessary and be able to fly home the same day.

When you search:

- allow yourself to go down the rabbit hole a bit. You never know what tidbits you are going to find.

- check on population and job growth

- see where there are infrastructure projects (e.g., highways/light rail projects);

- Check for:

  – Universities and university expansions
  – Redevelopment areas
  – Casinos
  – Military bases
  – Regional airports
  – Which areas are in high demand.
  – Company relocations (which employers are coming or going)

One trick I learned from my mentors, The Real Estate Guys, Robert Helms and Russell Gray, is to see what the big companies like Costco, Walmart, Home Depot, and McDonalds are doing. When they move into a residential real estate market, it's because they've been watching the numbers and expect growth.

They have the budgets to hire analysts that study migration trends, demographic shifts, infrastructure plans, etc. They check and see if there are major employers coming and if there are freeways, airports, and other key pieces of infrastructure to support a growing population.

When the signs look good these big companies move in to get ahead of growth. So, if you're seeing those types of companies moving into a residential market, it's a good bet that it's safe for you too.

After you have done all of the above, target a particular city as your market.

Once you target a particular city:

You'll need to look into job growth, population growth and other important market factors in a target city.

Comprehensive Annual Financial Report
One of the first places, if not *the* first place, to check is the Comprehensive Annual Financial Report (CAFR).

The CAFR is a city's financial report. It's a set of U.S. government financial statements comprising the financial report of a city (and other government entities) that adhere to the Governmental Accounting Standards Board (GASB). The GASB provides standards for the content of a CAFR in its annually updated publications.

A CAFR is prepared by a city and audited by an external accounting firm, so you can count on the accuracy of information contained in the CAFR.

To find your city's CAFR, you can simply google "City, State CAFR" and it should appear within the first few links. For example, if you would like the CAFR for Detroit, you'd do a google search for: "Detroit, Michigan CAFR."

If the CAFR does not appear at the top of the search page, you may have to drill down into the city's financial reports to find it. Some cities make it harder to find than others.

A CAFR is composed of three sections: Introductory, Financial, and Statistical, and each section provides an incredible amount of detailed information regarding the city's demographics, operations, management, plans for improvement, and more.

In the CAFR, you'll be able to see:

- population trends (are people coming or leaving the city? how old is the typical resident? What's the median income?)

- Unemployment rates

- The number of industries in the town.

- Universities in town (opens up options for student housing)

- How well the city is doing financially (you want a city that has a positive net position)

- and much more.

Where else do you look?

After you check out the CAFR, you can do google searches

-check local Chamber of Commerce sites

-check local business newspaper

-check sites/blogs of local commercial brokers

You want to be looking for signs of what is happening in employment and growth.

You can get a TREMENDOUS amount of information online. You can definitely find out through online searches if the fundamentals are there to explore further.

However, at the end of that online research, I believe it is necessary to put your feet on the ground in your future investment's location at least once.

Market Visits

If your online research signifies that the market looks promising, then it's time for a visit to the market.

Before you go: set up appointments with property managers, commercial brokers, commercial lenders, and even city officials (if possible - easier if you're doing big deals, tougher if you're doing small ones)

Kenny McElroy, author of the *ABCs of Real Estate Investing* recommends also setting up meetings with the publisher of the local apartment guide.

These meetings serve two major purposes:

*They will help you confirm your assumptions about the viability of a market or will show you were you were wrong

*Give you an opportunity to ask everyone you meet for recommendations of other team members & where to look to get more market information

Being in the city will give you a more accurate picture and allow you to narrow done to viable submarkets for your investment goals.

All this research is what you should do EVEN if you live in the market, and also every single time you're looking to buy something new. Things change: markets and submarkets go in and out of favor, big infrastructure projects (like light rail or highways) change the patterns and flows of a city.

***

Those are the 6 important factor for locating a profitable market, and how to find and assess it.

Once you have your market(s) picked, it is time to find your investment property. In the next chapter you will get information on how to find the right market for you.

Chapter Nine – Your Right Property

"Every person who invests in well-selected real estate in a growing section of a prosperous community adopts the surest and safest method of becoming independent, for real estate is the basis of wealth."
~Theodore Roosevelt, U.S. president

Once you find the right market and submarket, it's time to find the right property for you.

What's the right property? It depends upon your clear DESIRES and VISION.

The right property will deliver the benefits YOU desire and require.

Depending on your investing goals (whether it's finding a vacation rental for Airbnb or a multi-family dwelling or a shopping center or land for development), the property has to meet your requirements and serve towards your investment and lifestyle objectives.

Why is this important?

If you and your investment are a mismatch, you will be unsatisfied and possibly poorer for your efforts.

Make sure you have a clear sense of your desires. Go back to Chapter 6 if you need a refresher. Once you're clear, your object is to get the right property at the right price for you. It must be a fit.

How do you find a property that's a right fit for you?

There are three distinct, but important aspects to every property that will determine if it's a right fit:

(1) the physical characteristics of a property

(2) the purchase price

(3) the ownership situation.

Each of these items contributes an important facet to the nature of your investment and helps you answer the question of whether or not you are about to purchase the right property at the right price.

Note: For purposes of this chapter we're going to focus on the #1 most common asset types for real estate investors - residential (1-4) and residential multi-family (5+).

You will have many of the same considerations in other asset classes, and the right property will also be determined in reference to the physical characteristics, purchase price, and ownership situation. If you're investing in other asset classes, make sure you further your education though so that you will be able to know where the differences lie.

1. Physical Characteristics of the Property

Physical Aspects

When you're evaluating a property, start simple! Ask some basic questions about the property's physical aspects, including:

- How many units?
- How many bedrooms?
- How many bathrooms?
- What's the square footage?
- Is there a garage or a parking lot?
- Is there a back yard or other communal space?

The size and configuration of a building will determine what you can do with it (function) and purchase price.

Amenities

Make a list of the property's amenities. Ask yourself, "What extra amenities does the property have?"

- Dishwasher?
- Stainless steel appliances?
- Air conditioning?
- Laundry facilities?
- Pool?
- Community center?
- Gym?
- Barbecue?

- Dog park?

These extra amenities can add a great deal of value of a property *as long as they are in good working condition.* For example, having air conditioning could be great, but not if the old chiller system is broken or on its last legs (a very expensive fix).

Architecture

Evaluate the building's architecture. Ask yourself, "Does that architecture relate to the rest of the architecture on the block?" People will often pay a premium to live in building with desired architectural style & features.

In New York City, it might be a brownstone. In Los Angeles, craftsmen and mid-century modern are in demand. In New Orleans, a creole townhouse or French colonial style in the French Quarter might fetch you more rent.

In contrast, you might pay less (and perhaps get less rent) if you purchase a property that doesn't have the architectural style that's "in vogue." The 1970s building on a street where everything else is a sleek, newly-updated building will be relatively less valuable. As an investor, there may be an opportunity there, but you need to break down the numbers carefully. It depends on the desires of the market.

For example, I counseled a Real Estate Investor Goddess who was trying to purchase a property to use as a vacation rental in New Orleans. She was focused on getting an old property with lots of charm, but was frustrated because these architectural gems were snapped up as soon as they became available on the market, tended to be much more expensive, and often had a great deal of deferred maintenance.

In contrast, there were boxy, newer construction homes of similar location and size sitting on the market for thousands of dollars less.

I reminded her to think like the potential renter of a vacation rental and not like an owner-occupier. In vacation rentals, the most important things tend to be price and location.

On AirBnB, the person is generally looking for the best price they can find in the best location. They're usually more concerned with how close the property is to other things rather than to the property itself. If the inside is clean and visually appealing and the location is great, this will likely be an in-demand vacation rental even if it's not as charming on the outside.

She decided to pick one of the "boxy" houses up and got one for about $20,000 less than the French Colonial older homes she'd been looking at. This place didn't have the charm on the outside, but it was in great shape, so she undoubtedly saved more by not having to take care of any deferred maintenance. She modernized it a bit on the inside, got some great furniture, and it's now doing very well on AirBnB.

Class of Property

Often investors will talk about properties using class designations. Just as neighborhoods/areas have classes, so do buildings.

The class of the building is not necessarily the same class as the neighborhood. For example, you could have a C class building in an A neighborhood, or a B class building in a C neighborhood.

Here is a brief description of each property class:

Class A Properties

These properties represent the highest quality buildings in their market and area. They are generally newer properties built within the last 10-15 years and have modern amenities (granite countertops, hardwood floors, etc.), high-income earning tenants and low vacancy rates. Class A buildings are located in prime market locations and are typically professionally managed. Additionally, they usually demand the highest rent rates with little or no deferred maintenance issues. These are stable investments, but tend to provide lower cash flow.

Class B Properties

Class B investments are generally older than Class A (15-30 years). They tend to have relatively recent upgrades and modern appliances, amenities, etc. but may lack some of the "top-notch" amenities of a Class A property. Rental incomes in Class B properties tends to be lower than in a Class A, and you can expect higher maintenance costs due to the age of the property.

Mostly, these buildings are well maintained and many investors see them as a "value-add" investment opportunity because through renovation and common area improvements, the property can be upgraded to Class A or a Class B+. Buyers are generally able to acquire these properties at a higher Cap Rate (i.e., higher rate of return) than a comparable Class A property because these properties are viewed as riskier than Class A.

Class C Properties

Class C properties are typically more than 30 years old and located in less-than-desirable locations. These properties are generally in need of substantial renovations, including updating the building infrastructure to bring it up to date and possibly to code as well.

Class C buildings tend to have the lowest rental rates in a market with other Class A or Class B properties. Some Class C properties need significant repositioning, meaning that it may take some time before they get to steady cash flows for investors.

Class D Properties

Class D properties are old like a Class C, but with far more neglect. It's possible that a Class D building is uninhabitable. Class D buildings are generally extremely cheap, but can be very difficult and sometimes even dangerous to turn around and get good tenants in place.

Property Condition: Cosmetic Improvements vs. Deferred Maintenance

Ask yourself:

* What is the condition of the property?

* How much deferred maintenance is there?

* Does it look dated?

* Does it need new paint or flooring?

* Does it have very old and dingy bathrooms or kitchens?

I personally like investing in class B & C properties when they're in a neighborhood that's a class above, which is to say a Class B in a "A neighborhood" or a Class C in a "B neighborhood." Those are some of the best properties to upgrade intelligently and wisely to dramatically increase their value. I like taking an ugly duckling and making it into a swan.

Some words of wisdom if you're going that route: you want a diamond in the rough, but not too rough.

A great ugly duckling has good bones. The "invisible" features are solid. It has good plumbing, updated electrical, solid foundations, and a sound roof, but the visible features of the units are outdated. Basically, you need up clean it up and maybe upgrade a little bit. If you give the apartments a new paint job, new flooring, and some new appliances, the tenants will pay more rent. You'll have added to the income and therefore the value of the property by making thoughtful *cosmetic improvements*.

Cosmetic makeovers will typically add to the value of a property. People will generally pay more to live in a property that's more beautiful, upgraded, and has nicer amenities than the status quo (e.g., stainless steel vs. white appliances). However, they WON'T pay more rent because you've had to install a new roof, fix the plumbing, or repair the foundation. Those are necessary for habitability and must be done if they are needed, but tenants don't tend to see those improvements and they won't fetch you any extra money. So, watch out for **deferred maintenance.**

Proper due diligence is crucial to buying the right property. Check out the property thoroughly with educated professionals (inspectors/contractors) who can point out areas of concern BEFORE you buy. You can either negotiate a credit from the seller to fix it, have the seller fix it before closing, or decide to walk away from the property before you end up with a money pit.

Location

We already talked about in the last chapter about the importance of being in the right market and submarket. The micro-location of your property can affect its value too.

Think about what your ideal renter would like and look for. Here are a few things to consider.

Street Location

For an apartment building it's important for a building to have good **visibility** from the street - easy for tenants to spot and find. So, buying an apartment building on a busy street with lots of traffic could be great for an apartment investment. Most people who live in single-family homes, don't like to live on busy streets, however. So, a single-family rental on a busy street with lots of traffic will probably be less attractive and less valuable. In the case of a single-family rental, a corner lot on a quieter street may be more valuable to a renter.

Neighboring Properties

Think about what the neighbors are like, whether you are considering multifamily housing or a single-family residence. What are the neighboring properties like? If you're in a decent neighborhood, but you're next to a D-type building with bad elements living inside, this could affect who wants to live in your property. Most people don't want to live in a property with drugs and crime. They don't want to live next door to one, either.

Also, while you may not want the building right next door to the liquor store or other commercial venture in general, being next door to a Whole Foods could be a boon.

One of our complexes is across the street from a shopping center with a grocery store, a Starbuck's, and a Planet Fitness. This definitely adds to the desirability of the property.

Nearby Attractions

Now, think about entertainment. What are the attractions nearby? One of our apartment buildings is half a block from a nice park in one direction and a 5-minute walk from one of the toniest shopping centers in town in another direction. These definitely make the building more attractive. Proximity to attractions like beaches, parks, museums, shopping centers, etc., generally add to the value of a property.

Views

Take a look out the window. Does your property have special views? One of our rentals in Los Angeles rents at a premium because of its iconic view - it has great views of the Hollywood sign, the Griffith Park Observatory and Downtown LA. Generally, beautiful views increase the value of a property. Conversely, having a view of something unpleasant, like a landfill or a graveyard will likely decrease the value of the property or necessitate your finding a very specific type of tenant with very specific and somewhat unusual housing preferences.

2. Purchase Price

"In good deals the numbers work. In bad deals, they don't."
~Ken McElroy

When buying an investment property, you want to purchase a property that will give you a solid return on your investment. It's important that you pay the right price for your property. If you pay too much you won't make the returns you need even if the property is worth a great deal or has extremely attractive cash flow.

The numbers have to work. As Ken McElroy, author of the *ABCs of Property Investing* says, "In good deals the numbers work." So how do you tell if the numbers work? Let's talk about the how you determine the right value and price to pay.

The value of a property is calculated differently in a 1-4 unit vs. a 5+ unit property.

1-4 Unit Residential

In a 1-4 unit, an appraiser will determine the price by doing a comparative analysis of building of similar size and characteristics.

The appraiser will survey all similar buildings that have recently been sold in the area to determine the price.

For example, let's say you're buying a 2,200 square foot duplex (2-unit building). Each unit has 2 bedrooms and 1 bath. The appraiser will look at all the duplexes sold in the area - paying particular attention to the number of bedrooms, baths and similar amenities (e.g., pool, garage, backyard) and condition.

Based on the average price of other buildings sold, he or she will determine the price.

Rents are not factored into the appraised value of a property. The property could be empty, be rented out with above market rents, or be rented with below market rents. The appraised price would be the same.[17]

So how do you figure out if it's a good deal?

You're going to have to do some math.

Say you want to buy this duplex, and the asking price is $200,000.

Average rents in the market are $1,000/month for a 2-bedroom unit. That's a income of $2,000/month or total potential income of $24,000 per year.

Let's assume that your vacancy rate is 25%. Your total rental income will be $18,000/year.

Now you must figure your expenses. You want to factor in expenses like:

- repairs and maintenance,

- utilities (gas, water, electric),

- real estate taxes,

- insurance,

- replacement reserves (cash set aside for unexpected repairs - that broken air conditioner or roof repairs), and

- debt service/mortgage payments.

---

[17] Rents will be factored into your income as a borrower. For residential loans, 75% of the total fair market income can be counted towards income qualification of the borrower.

So how do you figure out what the mortgage payment will be?

We will talk more about how you get financing in the next chapter, Chapter 10, but for now you can figure out your mortgage loan payment quickly by going into Google and typing "mortgage payment." Enter in the loan amount (usually 75 - 80% of the total) and the interest rate.

Let's say that we expect to get a loan for 80% (you'll have a 20% down payment), the loan amount will be $160,000 ($200,000 x .80). With an interest rate of 4% and a 30-year loan, the monthly payment will be $764/month or $9168/year. Once you've figured out all of your costs and your likely annual income, it's time to factor in your financing.

Subtract your expenses from your income to realize your net operating income.

Total Income	$18,000
Less Total Expenses	-$14,888
Net Operating Income	$3,112

Net operating income (NOI) is $3,112/year or about $259/month. With a downpayment of $40,000, that means your yearly return on investment is 7.8%.

That return on investment will go up if you find ways to either decrease expenses (e.g. have the tenants pay all the utilities) or increase income (e.g. fix up the units by putting in nicer appliances and two-tone paint and start charging more rent).

So, is this a good investment? That depends on what works for you and what your desires are. It's definitely better than having your money in the bank right now, though, where it would probably be earning about 1/10th of a percent annually!

5+ Unit Buildings

Buildings of 5 or more units require a commercial loan, and the value of those buildings is determined differently. In commercial loans the value is determined by the current cash flow of the property. Whereas in a 1-4 unit property, rents do not play a role in the appraisal, in a 5+ unit, rents and cash flow are everything.

The value of a multifamily commercial building is determined by the net operating income (NOI) divided by the capitalization rate (Cap Rate).

Net Operating Income (NOI) means the total income minus total expenses.

Capitalization rate or **Cap Rate** is determined by the purchase price *trends* for a comparable building in the market. It's the average rate of return on investment in that market.

The value of the property = the NOI divided by the cap rate.

One other VERY IMPORTANT NOTE:

When assessing the NOI, make sure to look at the actual rent roll and the Trailing 12 ("T12") to determine income and expenses. The "trailing 12" is the income report for the 12 months immediately prior to the report date)

Many brokers can be a bit "fast and loose" with the numbers in their marketing materials. If you rely on those numbers in the brochure vs. actual numbers you will almost certainly be paying too much.

Income Determination

Income is determined by looking at actual rents (less vacancy), and also any other sources of income like laundry, pet fees, parking, etc.

Here's a simple example. This is a 6-unit property with 3 one-bedroom, one-bath units and 3 2-bedroom, one-bath units.

Rents:

# of Units	Type	Sq. Ft	Total sq. ft.	Rent	Total Rent	Rent/ Sq. Ft
3	1/1	650	1950	$600	$1,800	$0.92
3	2/1	750	2250	$725	$2,175	$0.97
6	Averages	675	4200	$662.5	$3,975	$0.95

The gross scheduled income for the property is $3975/month or $47,700 for the year.

Gross Scheduled Rent	$47,700
Less Vacancy (7%)	-$3,340
Net Rental Income	$44,060
Plus Other Income	$470
Total Income	$44,530

Expenses

Expenses include repairs and maintenance, utilities, taxes, insurance, property management, replacement reserves (fund you set aside of the inevitable capital items like appliances, carpets, countertops, roofs).

Repairs & Maintenance	$5,020
Utilities	$2,430
Real Estate Taxes	$3,900
Insurance	$720
Replacement Reserve	$1,200
Total Expenses	$13,270

Note, in this example, we are not putting in a property management line items. But if you plan on having professional property management (which I recommend if the property is larger and if it's not in the market where you live), you'd want to add that expense to your budget.

Net Operating Income

NOI equals the total income minus total expense.

Total Income	$44,530	
(Less) Expenses	-$13,270	
Net Operating Income	$31,260	

Property Value

The value is determined by the dividing the Net Operating Income (NOI) by the capitalization rate (cap rate).

If the cap rate in the market is 8%, to figure out the property value, divide the NOI $31,260 by .08 = $390,750. You should offer no more than this for the property.

The asking price may also go down if there are items of deferred maintenance to fix. For example, if the property needs a new roof, the buyer may lower the price or give you a credit for that.

Debt Service/Mortgage

After you have figured out the value of the property, you need to calculate the mortgage loan payment and your profit on your investment.

We will talk more about how you get financing in the next chapter, Chapter 10, but for now you can figure out your loan payment quickly by going into Google and typing "mortgage payment." Enter in the loan amount (usually 75 - 80% of the total) and the interest rate.

Let's say that we expect to get a loan for 80% (you'll have a 20% down payment), the loan amount will be $312,600 ($390,750 x . 80).

If the interest rate is 5% on a 30-year amortization, the loan amount will be $1678/month or $20,136/year.

Cash on Cash

Cash-on-cash return is the ratio of annual before-tax cash flow to the total amount of cash invested.

**cash-on-cash = annual before-tax cash flow
total amount invested**

To figure out the before-tax cash flow or total profit, subtract your debt service from the NOI. When you subtract that from the NOI of $31,260 that gives you a profit or before-tax cash flow of $11,124.

Net Operating Income	$31,260
Less Debt Service(Loan Payment)	-$20,136
Total Profit	$11,124

The original down payment/amount invested was $78,150.

To figure out your Cash on Cash, divide your profit by the downpayment.

Cash on Cash = $11,124/$78,150 = 14.23%

If you purchase this property for $390,750 for 20% down, your return on investment will be 14.23% per year. That's not bad!

As you increase the NOI (through rent increases and/or expense decreases) your yearly return on investment or cash-on-cash will increase as will the value of the property.

Remember one thing:

"In good deals the numbers work. In bad deals, they don't."

~Ken McElroy

If you go through this exercise and find that after expenses and debt service, you are NOT making a profit, or your return on investment is too low. That is a bad deal and this is not the right property to invest in.

3. Ownership Situation

When you talk about a property many people think about the first two aspects - the physical characteristics of a property (its location, state of repair or disrepair, size and functions, amenities, etc.) and the price (because the price you pay will determine whether or not it is a good investment).

Most people don't think about the third aspect: the ownership situation. The ownership situation has to do with who owns it, how they have been managing the property, and the owner(s)' motivations for selling. The ownership situation can determine a lot of the challenges or opportunities inherent in a purchasing a property.

Whether or not you *want* to think about it, it will be a necessary part of your purchase. You are purchasing a property from another human or humans. How they have been managing the property will affect the value of the property, and their own goals and motivations for selling will also play a big part in the sale.

Seller Motivation

One of the aspects of buying a property will be to assess the sellers' motivations for listing the property. A very motivated seller might be willing to take less on a property in exchange for speed in closing.

Negotiations will be different with an owner who's desperate to sell as quickly as possible versus an owner to someone who doesn't particularly want or need to sell.

Also, sometimes the owners are very clued in, savvy, and realistic about the value of their property. Other times owners think their properties are worth way more than they're worth.

If you are negotiating with someone who has a realistic sense of the value of their property, you can get the property and be creative while you do it.

When we bought our mobile home park in North Carolina, we bought the park from someone who had owned the park for 40+ years. Unfortunately, he was starting to have dementia and his children were very motivated to have him sell the park while the owner still had his wits about him.

The park had had very minimal management for years. It was in very poor shape and only 30% occupied. We were able to purchase the property at a great price and knew that because the market fundamentals were there, with good management and a decent upgrade of the space, the park would deliver an enormous return on investment.

Seller Management

Another aspect of the ownership situation has to do with how well an owner has been taking care of their property. A property with bad management presents a unique opportunity for value-add that is not always there. When it is, however, you can make dramatic changes in a property for the better relatively quickly. Improving the management is a surefire way to improve the financials of a property.

For example, in the 51-unit building we bought in Albuquerque, the ownership situation greatly affected the deal we were able to get.

First, the owners were a mom-and-pop organization that had let things get away from them, and the financials of the building were a mess. They also had let in all sorts of tenants (many of whom had stopped paying rent). The situation scared a lot of other buyers off, but that was also a golden opportunity for us.

We knew that by improving management - keeping good books, evicting tenants who weren't paying rent or were bad elements in the complex, adding income streams (e.g., making the building pet friendly and charging pet deposits), decreasing expenses (e.g., charging back utilities to tenants), we could add value to the building and create value for ourselves and our tenants.

When you're buying pay attention to the ownership situation and be open to opportunities showing up because of that.

***

If you find a property with the right physical characteristics and the right price for sale by the right buyer, you will be happy.

The next thing is to figure out how to buy it. In the next chapter, we will discuss the four different ways you can purchase your property (i.e., find the money).

Chapter Ten – Your Right Financing

"If you're not going to put money in real estate, where else?"
~Tamir Sapir, business mogul

"Ninety percent of all millionaires become so through owning real estate. More money has been made in real estate than in all industrial investments combined. The wise young man or wage earner of today invests his money in real estate."
~Andrew Carnegie

In this chapter, we are going to talk about the different ways you can finance or pay for a property. Why is this important? If you don't have the money, you don't have the deal.

There are 4 basic ways to finance a property:

1) **Use your own money:** pay all in cash.

2) **Get lender financing**: borrow money from a bank or hard money lender).

3) **Get seller financing:** instead of going to a bank, the property seller finances the property).

4) **Syndicate:** Invest with other people who all pool resources to purchase a property (syndication).

You can also acquire property through a combination of any of the above.

Let's look at each method one by one.

1. Use your own money - pay all in cash.

This is the simplest method. You find a property, agree to a purchase price with the seller. You have the money to pay for it outright, so you write a check and you own the property.

About one-third of all real estate transactions in the United States are purchased this way.[18]

When we were flipping properties, usually this was how we purchased properties.

The Benefits of Buying All Cash

• **Sellers are likely to favor buyers who can pay in cash.**
  Cash buyers are more definite and can close much faster. Sellers prefer this.

• **The home price may be reduced for you if you pay in full up front.** Buying in cash reduces a certain amount of uncertainty for a seller, so they often reduce the price for an all-cash buyer. You also have greater negotiating power regarding closing time, repairs, and more.

• **All-cash purchases streamline the home-buying process.**
  If you don't have to get a loan, that means less paperwork and no delays for mortgage approval.

• **You can can save a lot of money.**
  Cash buyers usually save on closing costs, bank appraisals, mortgage applications and fees, title insurance, and so on.

---

[18] http://realtormag.realtor.org/daily-news/2017/03/01/all-cash-sales-falling-nationwide

- **You eliminate the risk of loan denial.**
  Getting a mortgage can be a lengthy and cumbersome process and there are a lot of hurdles. My husband and I are self-employed. We had a lot of cash in the bank, but we had a hard time showing the income necessary to get a loan. It was much easier for us to pay all-cash for our flip properties.

- **You can have more peace of mind.**
  You never have to worry about losing your property because you can't afford to repay the mortgage loan. When you own the property 100%, you are not subject to any changes in interest rates and are not as susceptible to market fluctuations. Your property can never be foreclosed upon.

- **You gain full, immediate equity in the home.**
  With an all-cash payment, you immediately own 100% of the home.

- **You pay much less for the property in the long run.**
  No loans means no interest.

For example:
Let's say you find a duplex for sale and negotiate the price to $177,000. You could get a mortgage at an interest rate of 4%. Here's how much you would pay to own it outright in these 3 different scenarios:

1. **All-Cash Payment:** There's no math required on this one – you pay the sticker price of $177,000.

2. **15-Year Fixed Rate Mortgage (20% Down):** Including your 20% down payment, the total cost of a median priced $177,000 home, financed with a 15-year mortgage will have cost a total of $257,119 after 15 years of interest and principal payments.

3. **30-Year Fixed Rate Mortgage (20% Down):** Including your 20% down payment, the total cost of this $177,000 home, after 30 years of interest and principal payments will cost $375,425.

As you can see from the above scenario, over time you may end up paying more than double the price because you have been paying interest.

Downsides of Buying All Cash

- **Loss of Liquidity**
Money put into a property is not liquid (i.e., it's not easily accessible), and generally a property is a fairly expensive asset. If you pay that much money for anything upfront, it is going to cost you a great deal of liquid assets in the form of cash. Cash tied up in real estate is not easily tapped in the case of financial troubles, except through a sale or cash-out refinance. So, you should only buy a home outright if you are still able to have a comfortable cushion of cash for emergencies.

- **Lack of Leverage**
Although most of us are in a hurry to pay off debt, having debt (i.e., being leveraged) in real estate can actually be one area where there is an upside. First, you can use buy many more properties with the same amount of cash. If you buy homes with 20% down, you can buy five $100,000 homes with a mortgage versus only one all cash. Also, if you get a very favorable interest rate, you may actually make money by having a mortgage due to the effects of inflation.

- **No Mortgage Interest Tax Advantage**
Under the American tax code, the tax treatment of mortgage interest is one of the biggest incentives for many property owners. Buying a property with cash will not provide any such tax deductions.

2. Get lender financing (i.e., borrow money from a bank or hard money lender)

The most popular way to finance a property is to get a loan from a lending institution.

It works like this: you find a property, and then apply for a loan for the money to cover some or all of the cost to purchase the property.[19] The loan on a property is called a mortgage. Every month you pay back the interest and some of the principal on your loan.[20]

As we talked about in the last chapter, there are residential loans (for 1-4 unit residential buildings) and commercial loans (for every other type of real estate: 5+ units, retail, industrial, hotels, land, etc.).

Key Differences Between Residential and Commercial Loans

a) Who can borrow?

Residential Loans

In residential loans only individuals can borrow.

The banks will look to the income, credit, and debt of the borrower to assess if they are financially fit enough to get a mortgage.

Banks want to make sure that you have the **income** to pay for the mortgage. They generally want your mortgage payment to be no

---

[19] Depending on circumstances downpayment can be 0% [e.g., Veteran's Association Loans], 3% [e.g., FHA Loans, for first time homebuyers]. See our "How to Purchase for Little to No Money Down" webinar to learn more about some of these loans types.

[20] There are interest-only mortgages where the principal balance is not paid-down.

more than 30% of your gross monthly income. They will also check to see about the source of the income. Typically, they prefer that you've been in the same job for over 2 years. This is evidence of your financial stability. For self-employed professionals, you need to show two years of tax returns and sufficient income for a loan.

With regards to **credit**, banks typically look for a FICO score of over 720 to access the best rates. You may still qualify for a mortgage with a lower credit score, but you will pay higher rates. If your score is below 620, you may need a much higher down payment and/or may be denied.

Banks will assess your **debt-to-income ratio**. In other words, they want to know what your total debt (including car loans, credit cards bills, student loans, etc.) is in relation to your gross monthly income. Your debt-to-income ratio should generally be no more than 36% of your gross income. If it's too high, consider paying down your credit cards and other debts.

Commercial Loans

In commercial loans, entities (e.g., Limited Liability Corporations (LLCs)) can also purchase the property and borrow money in order to do so.

Why is that important? An entity can provide certain layers of liability protections for the owners. So, for example, if someone slips and falls on your property, you will not personally be liable.[21]

There are also certain tax benefits to using an entity. For example, an entity may pay income taxes at a lower rate and/or be entitled to take more deductions. Talk to your CPA to figure out the best way for you to purchase a property.

---

[21] I need to qualify that statement - you wont pay as long as you didn't push or trip them or in any other way directly cause them to slip and fall. If you were a direct cause of an accident, the entity protections will not apply.

The banks will also look at the individuals within the entity. They consider the net worth, liquidity and experience of the members of the LLC.

Within the LLC, one of the signatories on the loan must have a **net worth** of at least the value of the loan.

The LLC member(s) need to have **liquidity** generally representing at least 20% of the loan.

The LLC member(s) must also evidence **experience** with running that type of business. A bank is unlikely to give you a loan to run a 100-unit apartment building, if you've only ever owned a couple single family rentals. If you have a team member that has successfully run a 60-unit apartment building however, the bank will consider the experience of your team member. You can also overcome this experience deficit by partnering with an experienced and well-regarded property manager in the market where you're purchasing the property.

The benefit of this type of arrangement is that you personally don't have to have all of these factors. You can partner with those who do.

For example, we syndicated a $3,075,000 77-unit apartment building. We did not have that net worth. We did not have 20% ($615,000) sitting in the bank, and we had never owned/ managed an apartment building before. Fortunately, we were able to partner with others who met these requirements. We found someone with the financial requirements we needed. We added her to the loan as a principal guarantor or "key principal." She's not managing the asset, but she has her name on the loan.

Why would she want to do that? It's given her experience on the loan. The next time if she wants to get her own loan, she has previous experience and can probably access a non-recourse[22] loan because of it.

Then we partnered with our partner Chris, a great guy who had successfully raised $5,000,000 for the syndication of a 122-unit building in Dallas, and was managing that property. We found the deal, so he was happy to join forces and bring his experience to it.

b) Whose income matters?

Residential Loan

For a residential loan, the bank looks at the personal gross income of the borrower vs. the amount of debt they owe.

As a rule of thumb, your total debt should be no more than 45% of your gross income and your mortgage payment should be no more than 28%.

Commercial Loan

For a commercial loan, the income of the property itself is what matters most. The bank will look at the net operating income (NOI) of the property. [See previous chapter for a description of how the NOI is calculated]. The bank will also consider the **Debt Service Coverage Ratio (DSCR)**.

The DSCR is the ratio of the net operating income to the proposed mortgage debt service on an annual basis. It has to do with the available cash after debt payments are made. .

----

[22] A non-recourse loan, as opposed to a recourse loan, is one that doesn't have a personal guarantee on the loan. In other words, if you default on a non-recourse loan, the bank can take over the building but cannot come after you personally. In a recourse loan, the bank can come after your other assets to be made whole

Banks look at this because they want you to be successful in your real estate business! If you don't make enough income to pay off the debts and make a profit, you won't be successful and they'll have to foreclose upon you. No one wants that! Banks want to hold money, not physical property.

So most lenders want a minimum DSCR of 1.20x.

To calculate the DSCR simple divide the NOI by the annual debt.

In our commercial loan example from the last chapter, the DSCR was 31,250 / 20,136 = 1.55. Most lenders would be happy with that.

c) What's the mortgage term?

This is variable, but in general residential loans are for much longer terms. A typical residential mortgage length term is for 30 years. A typical commercial mortgage term is 10 years.

d) Are there pre-payment penalties?

Residential loans can almost always be paid off at any time, regardless of the payout term lengths, without any penalty. Furthermore, residential borrowers often choose to refinance when interest rates drop, which is much harder to do when a loan has prepayment penalties.

Commercial real estate loans typically do have prepayment penalties. Often the commercial loan prepayment penalty is on a sliding scale, growing smaller as a percentage of the loan each year.

For example, on one of our commercial loans the prepayment penalty on years one to three is 3%, on year 4, it's 2%, on years five to 10, it's 1%. On a $5 million-dollar loan, this percentage amount makes a big difference. Each percentage point represents an extra $50,000 in penalty.

While commercial loans are shorter in term, they are less flexible during the term of the loan than are residential loans. If you have this kind of loan, you will have to refinance the loan at the end of its term, sell the property, or pay the amount in full. Depending on the loan, you may have to pay a prepayment penalty if you refinance early.

3. Seller Financing

Seller financing is when, instead of getting a loan from a bank, the buyer gets a loan from the seller for the purchase.

Seller financing is often structured like a traditional residential mortgage except the seller plays the role of "the bank" and receives monthly payments of interest and principal from the buyer along, in most cases, with some form of down payment. In the event that borrower fails to make the payments, the seller can foreclose and claim the collateral, usually the property on which the loan was made, much as the bank would have.

In the case of seller financing, the buyer and seller will execute a promissory note providing an interest rate, repayment schedule, and consequences of default. The buyer will send the monthly mortgage payments to the seller, until the loan is paid off.

Seller financing is common where conventional mortgages are hard to come by. Sometimes this is because of a down market and sometimes this is because of the unusual nature of the asset class or particularities of the property. Seller financing allows you to be flexible and find win-win situations.

Our story of seller financing:
Our mobile home park was purchased through seller financing. It was a $600,000 purchase from an older seller who was wanting to get the property sold quickly.

The down payment was quite high - 47% and the loan is only for 5 years. The price was incredibly good for the type of asset, so it made sense to us as buyers to go this route.

For the seller, it made sense too. A buyer would have a very hard time getting a loan on his property. In general, commercial loans under $1,000,000 are challenging to get. Also, this property was in really bad shape - only about 1/3 occupied and needing a lot of work. It would have been tough to get the appraisal value we needed. Our partners saw the diamond in the rough and went for it though.

It was a win-win for all.

Here's another example:

I recently interviewed Lanisha Stubbs, a real estate investor and broker here in Los Angeles, who makes frequent use of seller financing. She shared with me one great example of a time she used seller financing.

While walking through her neighborhood, she discovered a pretty run-down fourplex occupied by a man and his cousin. The two had inherited this 4-unit building in Los Angeles and owned it outright, so they had 100% equity in the building. They were stuck though. The building was in terrible condition. They lived in one dingy unit, the other three units were practically uninhabitable. The men were not working, so unable to get a refinance on the property, and they did not have the cash to fix it up.

She recognized they had a problem and she could help them fix it. She offered to become 50/50 owners with them on the property. In exchange for her 50% stake, she would pay to have the property fixed up. She was able to get financing for the remodel with no money down and fixed up the other units -- while these men stayed living on the property and still had a home.

As the units are fixed up, they are being rented. After her costs to fix up the units are paid back, she will share the rental profits with the owners/now her partners. Now these men have a property that is worth 3 times what it was before, they are receiving income, and they live in a fixed-up unit. Lanisha is the 50% owner of a fourplex now worth $1.3 million, receives monthly rental income, and accomplished all of this with no money out of her own pocket.

That's pretty awesome!

Seller Financing Advantages for Buyers

• **Good when a conventional loan is unavailable**
For some buyers it may be hard to get a conventional loan. Your financial situation may not fit into neat little boxes - perhaps you don't have a predictable W-2 job and income, a stable employment history, or a good credit score. Sellers can be more flexible and creative than a bank, and allow for a buyer's unique circumstances.

• **The closing process can be faster**
You don't have to wait for all the approvals that you would need in a bank.

• **Closing costs are lower**
You do not have to pay bank or appraisal fees.

• **The down payment amount can be extremely flexible**
It can be whatever you and the seller agree to.

Seller Financing Disadvantages for Buyers

• **Mortgage period is often much shorter**
The mortgage period is shorter (e.g., 5 years versus 30 years), so there may be higher monthly payments or there can be a big balloon payment at the end of the term (hopefully buyers can refinance before that point).

- **Typically higher interest rates than a bank would offer**
  This is an unusual type of loan and it is often in high demand. The market often allows sellers willing to offer seller financing the ability to charge higher interest rates than market rate.

- **Buyers still need to prove that they're credit-worthy**
  In most cases, a seller still will want some evidence that making a loan to you is a good idea. Many default to credit rating, although in real estate sometimes they will simply want to insure that they are able to foreclose on the property without a loss if you fall delinquent.

- **Buyer needs to make sure that the seller owns the property free and clear**
  Your due diligence duty becomes even more important because it will be up to you, not the bank, to make sure that the title on the property is unclouded. Fail in this and you might be buying yourself some legal troubles.

Seller Financing Advantages for Sellers

- **Minimize carrying costs while waiting for the perfect buyer**
  Seller financing opens up the pool to more buyers, which may lead to a quicker sale and therefore less carrying costs.

- **Can get the deal done much more quickly**
  Without all the hoops of getting bank financing, a seller-financing deal may get done much more quickly.

- **Will distinguish the property from other listings**
  Offering seller financing can help you get a property sold faster (especially in a down market).

- **Increase the possibility of getting the full asking price**
  Because seller financing is an attractive option for buyers, you will likely be able to charge more if you are offering it.

- **May get a down payment to buy another property**
  You can simply require the down payment on the property you

are seller financing to be enough o make a down payment on your next purchase.

- **Can ditch any monthly expense associated with owning the property**
Seller financing offers the attraction of monthly payments (like rent) but without the hassles of property maintenance or property taxes. Just remember, at the end of the term of the note, if the borrower meets the requirements they will own the property, unlike a renter.

Seller Financing Disadvantages for a Seller

- **Don't get the full proceeds from the property at once**

- **Have to make sure the buyer is credit-worthy** - You can "hedge your bets" in this regard by making sure that the collateral is worth more than the loan.

4. Invest with other people who all pool resources to purchase a property (Syndication)

Syndication is a great option that allows you to leverage other people's money (OPM) and in some cases other people's time (OPT) to acquire more property than you could by yourself.

Syndication can be used with any of the other three methods. You can use a syndication to purchase a property all cash, to purchase with lender financing, or to purchase with seller financing.

Within syndication there are two major roles: the active investor/sponsor/syndicator and the passive investor.

Active Investor/Sponsor/Syndicator

The **active investor, sponsor or syndicator** (these terms are used interchangeably) is the person that is arranging the syndication. They bring together the investors to collectively purchase the property.

Typically, they will find the deal, structure it, enroll investors, collect the money, and then manage the asset afterwards.

A syndicator is not necessarily acting as a property manager, but they will need to manage the property manager(s) and other aspects of the deal (e.g., get insurance for the property, make sure that necessary rehabs are done, ensure taxes are done for the entities and K-1s are provided each year to investors, etc.)

NOTE: PRACTICE SAFE SYNDICATION. In the United States, if you take other people's money and are managing it, this will fall under U.S. Securities Law. If you want to do this type of transaction, you MUST engage the services of a good securities attorney and file the proper paperwork. If you ignore this advice you could end up paying huge fees or even seeing some jail time. So, CONTACT A SECURITIES ATTORNEY BEFORE SYNDICATING.

Benefits for Syndicator

- **You leverage other people's money** to buy an investment property that may be much more than what you could afford by yourself

- **You receive a portion of the equity and cash flow** in exchange for the time and energy placed into syndicating and managing the deal. You can structure a deal so that you have a substantial ownership stake in a property with very little or none of your own capital

- **It's very win-win** You set up an investment vehicle that benefits tenants, other investors, and other team members.

- **You have management control** of the asset.

*NOTE: you can partner with other syndicators and be a sponsorship team. I recommend this approach and this is how I do it myself. As a team, you split the responsibilities and the rewards.

Downsides for Syndicators

- **Not very passive income** - active investor needs to find the deal, find investors, manage the property or the property manager, and manage the syndication. This can be a lot of work - especially up front.

- **The sponsor may need to front a lot of cash and time up front** This allocation of resources may not always pay off (for example, the deal you spent months pursuing and working on may not close in the end).

Passive Investor

The passive investor is a person who invests in the syndication. They do not manage the property. They put in their investment and just wait for returns. It's analogous to investing in stock. If you invest in some General Electric stock, you own a piece of the company, but you don't get to manage it or have a say in what happens to the company on a day to day basis.

Example:

A real estate investor Goddess named Sonya had $125,000 in an IRA account and $25,000 in savings. She wanted her money to work better for her and be a real estate investor, but she didn't have the time or desire to find and manage a property.

Sonya passively invested in a 314-unit building in Dallas, TX. She passively invested $50,000 from her self-directed IRA (SD-IRA) account and is one of 29 investors in the deal. She is earning an average 11.5% cash-on-cash return on her money and when the building is turned-around and sold in 5 years, it's projected that she will have doubled her total investment.

Note: In this example, Sonya invested with her SD-IRA. This is a great vehicle for investing in real estate passively. We talk more about self-directed retirement accounts in Chapter 7.

Benefits of Being a Passive Investor

* **Leverage OPM and OPT** to invest in a property that is much more than what you could afford or manage by yourself.

* **It's a truly passive investment** - All you have to do is write your initial check to get into the investment and then cash your checks as your money is returned to you with friends.

Downside of Being a Passive Investor

* **No control over the management of the property** - For some people that's a benefit. It is important that the syndicators/active investors do a good job though.

* **You need to have the money to invest** - Minimum investments in these types of deals can vary tremendously - from $1,000 on crowd funding sites to upwards of $100,000.

Sometimes having the money to invest, means you need to have enough net worth or income to be considered an **accredited investor**.

An "accredited investor" is defined as a person or couple with $1,000,000+ net worth (not including their personal residence) OR a yearly income of $200,000+ (for an individual) or $300,000+ (for a couple). With the income requirement, you must have had this income for 2 or more years and have a reasonable expectation of maintaining that level of income in the coming year.

If you are not an accredited investor, don't despair. There are many opportunities for non-accredited investors to invest in syndications.

***

In summary, here are the 4 ways to pay for your investment properties:

1) Use your own money - pay 100% all cash.

2) Get lender financing (i.e., borrow money from a bank or hard money lender).

3) Get seller financing - (i.e, instead of going to a bank, the property seller finances the property

4) Invest with other people who all pool resources to purchase a property (syndication).

Which way(s) is most interesting to you? Why?

_____
_____
_____
_____
_____

What are the steps you need to take to prepare yourself to purchase?

_____

_____

_____

_____

_____

_____

_____

_____

_____

Chapter Eleven – The Goddess Secret Sauce: Pleasure, Intuition & Sisterhood

"The best fertilizers you can find for your sprouting desires are fun and pleasure- they are all-natural and you can never have too much of them, so sprinkle them daily throughout your life." ~Regena Thomashauer

This chapter is it. **This is the secret sauce for women investors.**

This is where you find the rocket fuel for your desires. This is where you find your ability to quantum leap. This is where the magic happens.

The rest of the Real Estate Investor Goddess Investing Framework is about the nuts and bolts of real estate investing. It's all very important and necessary, and if you lose any piece of the framework, it will all fall apart.

BUT, this is what will make things show up with relative ease. This is what distinguishes real estate investing from real estate investing like a Goddess.

When people ask how we found our properties in Albuquerque, I sometimes give a more complicated answer than what happened. I'll talk about how we assessed the market and built the team, but that's not quite an honest answer.

The honest answer is that my husband and I were completely guided to it. As if by magic, we met a woman at a networking event who told us about Albuquerque. She introduced us to our broker (he was her nephew). My husband did research to confirm what we were guided towards, but I mostly just trusted that sense inside that told me "Yes, this is it."

With relative ease and grace, we were able to acquire two buildings under asking price even though we were new in the market and were not the highest bidders. It was a financial miracle.

This, I believe is the power we have as women. And we can heighten that power to invite in what we desire with the 3 factors of the Goddess Secret Sauce:

1. Pleasure

2. Following Your Intuition

3. Sisterhood.

Pleasure

"Pleasure in the job puts perfection in the work."
~Aristotle

Pleasure is the first part of the secret sauce. For women, it is CRUCIAL to follow your pleasure. If you find that you have to "man up" or "muscle through" something, almost certainly you're NOT going to be happy with the results.

It's not to say that you will never need to work or to engage in things you would rather not be doing. If that were the case, I would never commute anywhere, help my daughter with her homework, work on my taxes, etc.

You still need to do the work, but adding pleasure to your life/real estate investing will help make the journey a joy.

3 Steps to Add Pleasure to Your Real Estate Investing:

There are 3 ways to add pleasure to your real estate investing. I call these the 3 Blissciplines:

1) **Do at least one pleasurable activity every day.**
   It doesn't have to be real estate related. Maybe it's getting a manicure or massage. Maybe it's sitting in the sun and meditating. Maybe it's watching your favorite movie. Maybe it's having a great make-out session with your honey. Maybe it is going to open houses (I find that very pleasurable). Whatever it is, do at least one pleasurable thing every day. This daily dose of Vitamin P will invite in magic and miracles into your life.

2) **Make sure that the activities you are doing are leading to pleasurable results in your life.**
   Always ask yourself (especially if you're about to do something that's not usually pleasurable): will this activity lead to a pleasurable result in my life? I may not like getting onto the Los Angeles freeways to drive 90 minutes to speak at an event, but I know at the end of the road I'm going to be able to do something that brings me an incredible amount of joy. I will also happily drive to spend time with my favorite girlfriends or to visit a fun new spot.

   If I have to get into traffic to meet someone that always drains my energy, then it's a no go. It's not leading to a pleasurable result, so it's not going to happen.

With regards to real estate, you may not want to do underwriting for an investment, but if it will lead to the pleasurable result of having your money working for you and coming back to you with friends while you sleep, vacation, or watch television, then you do it.
However, if it's extremely un-pleasurable to do it and it's going to lead to a world of frustration for you, then have someone else do it. I personally don't like doing underwriting. It's not at all pleasurable for me. I let my husband do it because it's something he enjoys more.

I, on the other hand, love design and could spend hours finding the perfect light fixture for the kitchens. My hubby would rather watch paint dry, so that's my job.

You want to have the pleasurable result, but it's even better to have pleasure in the doing. Focus on doing the activities that actually bring you pleasure, that feel easy, that bring you to flow. Other activities that you'd rather not be doing should be done by others whenever possible.

3) Add pleasure to what might otherwise be an un-pleasurable activity

I know I have to wash the dishes, but I can put on my favorite tunes and put on my tiara and a tutu while I'm doing it. All of a sudden, it's pretty fun. I can get others to help me too, and now it's a party.

When I have to do a long drive, I get some great tunes, podcasts[23] and/or audiobooks to listen to for the drive. I will stop at Starbucks and get my favorite coffee drink and savor it

---

[23] Listen to the Real Estate Investor Goddesses podcast for some pleasurable listening. :)

on the drive. Whenever possible, I will find someone else to drive with me - it makes it more fun and allows us to use the carpool lanes.

Those are the three ways to infuse pleasure into your life.

Understand that Pleasure ≠ Comfort!

Being "in pleasure" is *not* the same as being in your comfort zone. Going after your pleasure is often a radical act that will often require you to get outside of your comfort zone.

The reason going for your pleasure will often require you to step outside of your comfort zone is because you have been conditioned against going after your pleasure.

Why You Will Likely Have to Fight For Your Pleasure

There's a part of you that's going to rebel against this. This is your inner ego voice, and it may fight you tooth and nail.

It's going to say: "Good girls don't do this!" You may have been taught that if it feels good it's sinful. Your ego will tell you that you are wrong for even wanting to do this.

It's going to say that "this is frivolous." "I'm too busy for this nonsense." "I don't have time for pleasure." "I can't take time for pleasure when there's dinner to be put on the table."

You've probably been taught "no pain, no gain." You've probably been taught about the Puritan work ethic and that there is virtue in the struggle. You've probably been taught you've got to "put your nose to the grindstone" and work no matter what.

Your inner ego voice is going to say that "prioritizing your pleasure is selfish." "You can do this, but only after others are fed, homework is done, work assignments are finished, etc."

You've also probably been taught to be a nurturer and a caregiver and to put everyone else's needs before your own.

Trust me, when I say what your inner ego voice is saying isn't true. It's definitely not true for women. It's time to let go of those old beliefs.

Trust me though when I say, pleasure will result in you having better results in less time, and generally just leave you and everyone around you happier.

Ignore the voice that's rebelling against this and commit to pleasure like *it's your job. Make it a priority.*

Do it because you're actually going to enjoy yourself - and that's reward enough. Life is meant to be fun. These blissciplines will help ensure that it's fun.

Do it because you're too busy not to do it. When you're in your pleasure, you will magnetize things to you and it will save you time that you would have otherwise spent struggling to muscle through.

Do it because if you're not pleasured – if you're stressed, overworked and overwhelmed — you're going to attract more people and situations that stress and overwhelm you.

Do it because prioritizing your pleasure, is one of the most generous things you can do for others. When you're happy, you can help make everyone else around you happy.

I know that first hand. I learned the importance of pleasure by observing my mom. It feels very vulnerable to share this story, but I'm going to share it here because it's the reason that I'm so passionate about women staying pleasured - especially moms.

This story didn't start out too happily, if I have to be honest.

When I was very little we lived in the country of Ivory Coast. My family moved to the United States when I was 5. My mom got a pretty good job at the World Bank as an administrative assistant, but for a long time my dad could not find work. My mother was the only breadwinner for a family of 5 (soon it became 6 when my little sister was born one year after we moved).

At that time, my mom's habit was to put herself last. Her pleasure wasn't even on the to-do list. She did not take time to deal with her health or her happiness, and she was miserable.

My memories of her at that time were of a raging banshee – furious and frustrated at everything. My dad did eventually get a job, but he was definitely underemployed for his level of education. My mom remained miserable and very ill-tempered.

I understand now it must have been incredibly stressful for her, but as a young girl all I understood was that this screaming, angry, stressed out woman scared me. I turned to my dad for nurturing and support. With my mom, I just tried to stay out of her way and her temper.

When I was 12, my parents separated. My brothers lived with my dad and my sister and I lived with my mom.

Something miraculous happened during that separation.

My mother went to therapy and she learned something. She learned to prioritize herself and her pleasure. She started to get her hair and nails done regularly. She joined Weight Watchers and started working out. She lost 50 lbs and looked great, but more importantly she became happy.

The wonderful woman she was underneath all that frustration and anger (because other people weren't doing what she wanted them to do to make her happy), came out when she realized that other people *couldn't* make her happy. That was her job. When she became more selfish about ensuring her needs were met first and prioritizing pleasure, she became a way better mom. She was more loving, patient, and better able to meet our needs. She also became a better employee and got a series of raises and promotions.

After a year and a half my parents reconciled. They were and still are happier than ever. Their separation was more than 30 years ago and they celebrated their 50th wedding anniversary last November. They're more in love now than ever, and all four of us kids are incredibly close with our mom.

From my experience observing my mom's transformation, I learned the truth of "Happy Mom, Happy Family." I learned how prioritizing your own pleasure and maintaining your happiness is a gift you gift to those around you.

It is CRITICAL that women take time to ensure they stay healthy, happy, and pleasured. Sometimes the most *selfless* thing you can do is be *selfish* enough to be in your pleasure.

If you are pleasured, the people that are already in your life will be happier, and you're going to attract people and opportunities that will add to the pleasure in your life. It creates a virtuous cycle of goodness and wonder.

What do you have to lose? Nothing!

So what are you doing to be in your pleasure today?

Make a list of 30+ things that bring you pleasure - they can be free or uber-luxurious, or anything in between, and commit to doing at least one a day.

Some items on my list are (not listed in any particular order): bubble baths, going to the beach and sticking my toes in the sand, massage, facial, mani-pedi, hiking with one of my BFFs, yoga class, snuggling with my puppy, kids, and/or hubby, travel (give me a suitcase and a plane ticket to just about anywhere and I'll be happy), sex, painting, meditating, dancing, and so much more.

Now it's time to make your list. List things that make you feel pleasured:

1. _____

2. _____

3. _____

4. _____

5. _____

6. _____

7. _____

8. _____

9. _____

10. _____

11. _____

12. _____

13. _____

14. _____

15. _____

16. _____

17. _____

18._____

19._____

20._____

21._____

22._____

23._____

24._____

25._____

26._____

27._____

28._____

29._____

30._____

Now that you have a list, commit to doing at least one pleasurable activity per day.

Intuition

"The intuitive mind is a sacred gift and the rational mind is a faithful servant. We have created a society that honors the servant and has forgotten the gift." ~Albert Einstein

Your intuition is the second part of the Goddess secret sauce. It's particularly strong for most women, and it's one of our most powerful tools. I call it the GPS for your life.

Have you ever had an intuitive sense about someone or something? Maybe you heard a voice that steered you in the right direction? Or you "just knew" something was the right decision or you knew that it was wrong?

Several years ago, I had an instant liking to a man I met on a blind date. I felt a strong feeling for him even before he spoke. I "just knew" instantly. That man is now my husband.

Intuition is very real, and tends to be particularly strong in women. It's a gift that we have, and it's extremely valuable for your investing (or anything else in your life).

What Is Your Intuition?

Your intuition is the culmination of various instantaneous mental processes including: automatic processing, subliminal priming, implicit memory, heuristics, right-brain processing, instant emotions, nonverbal communication and creativity.

It's based on facts filed just below the conscious level.

Right now, you may be focused on reading this book, but your ears, eyes, skin, nose are picking up on all sorts of cues that are filed subconsciously - you're hearing external noises (maybe traffic outside or the birds chirping), you're sensing subtle temperature changes, you're seeing things happening in the periphery.

On a conscious level, you're only picking up about 5% of what's happening around you. Your subconscious is picking up the other 95%. Your intuitive guidance is based on this fuller level of information stored in your subconscious.

Intuitive guidance will come to you in different ways. Sometimes it's like a sudden bolt, sometimes it's subtler.

It may come through sight, sound, physical sensations in your body, or through "just knowing" information, or a combination of any or all of the above.

My mentor Robert Helms says that every time he is the right buyer for a deal, he "just knows it." Even if there are a dozen other offers, his intuition will let him know that it is his. He doesn't worry about the others, because when he gets that sensation he knows that his offer will be accepted and he will become the next owner.

This is the same sense and knowing that told me "yes, this is it" about Albuquerque, New Mexico. That same voice told me "yes" to the broker, "yes" to the property management company, "yes" to the lender, etc.

Trusting that guidance allowed us to acquire two buildings under asking price even though we were new in the market and were not the highest bidders.

Following your intuition will always ease your path.

5 Steps to Hone Your Intuition:

1. Accept that intuition exists and can help you to reach your goals faster and more smoothly.

This is the key. Many people receive intuitive hunches all the time, but they ignore them because they do not believe or do not want to believe that intuition exists. Intuition is very real and listening to your intuition can have big pay-offs. A recent study showed that executives with the highest precognitive ability (intuitive perception) had on average 30% highest profit records than the ones who did not consider themselves intuitive.

2. Learn how to receive your intuitive guidance.

There are some common fears that come up for people around using their intuition. Some are: you can't trust it or you are not sure if the voice you're hearing is truly your intuitive guidance.

- **You can trust this voice/knowing.** Sometimes we hear a still small voice in our head that is our intuition. Sometimes we hear other voices that represent our fear and ego. How can you tell the difference?

  Almost always, your intuition is the *first* voice you hear. The fear is the one that tries to convince you that the first voice was wrong. If your intuition says, "Don't trust this person," the other voice may say things like "But so-and-so recommended her" or "But he's accomplished so much. Who am I not to trust him?"

  Also, the voice of fear/ego will rely on external support - what other people have said, what you read in the news, their awards received, their resume. The voice of intuition won't rely on anything - it will just assert itself. All it goes by is its own knowing.

  Lastly, intuition will never try to argue its case. Fear/ego will rely on logic. Fear and ego will give you very compelling reasons to ignore your intuition. Just know that if you're receiving "reasons," it's not your intuitive guidance.

- **Body Wisdom.** You will often feel your intuitive guidance in your body – there is a reason it's called your gut instincts. Your intuitive guidance is often felt in the stomach. You may also feel it in your heart, your throat, your head, and even your genitals.

  You can test it out. Ask a question and notice how your body reacts to two different outcomes. Normally, if it's intuitively a good thing you'll feel warmth, lightness, expansion. If it's intuitively a bad thing you'll feel heaviness, darkness, constriction. Again, you may feel it in different parts of your body.

3. Follow your intuition.

When you hear that still, small voice or you have inspired thought, act on it. This is really the most important step. If you need to, start practicing with small things -- what should you eat, which movie should you see, etc. After you've tried out your intuitive sense on smaller things, then you can start trusting your intuition to help you with more important decisions and actions. Which investment to make? Which property management company to hire?

Keep a journal so that you may be able to see patterns that emerge when you have intuitive thought.

4. Take care of your mind, body and spirit.

Exercise regularly, eat healthy foods, drink plenty of fresh water, and get adequate rest. The better you take care of yourself, the more receptive you will be to intuitive thoughts.

5. Make a practice of having some quiet/meditative time.

If you're always rushing about, over-thinking, and overwrought, it's going to be hard for you to hear your intuitive guidance. Make a habit of giving yourself some quiet contemplative time to hear your inner guidance.

Sisterhood

"So, if you want to flourish in your business and fully express your purpose, you need to make a conscious choice to be in sisterhood with similar manifestation Goddesses. It's science." ~ Bri Seeley & Thaís Sky, The Amplify Collective

Last, but certainly not least, sisterhood is part of the Goddess secret sauce.

Being in sisterhood is vitally important for a woman and invites magic into her life.

Sisterhood is more than just hanging out with your girlfriends and your female family members. Sisterhood is about a group of intention-setting women who come together with the purpose of supporting, celebrating, honoring, and inspiring one another.

Women Are Wired to Be Around Other Women

There are several studies that highlight how biologically women are wired to be around other women.

Being around other women feels good. One of nature's "feel good" hormones - Oxytocin, the "bonding hormone", is released in women's brains in 3 instances: during sex, during breast feeding, and when women are in groups of other women. Nature has us wired to bond with our lovers, our babies, and other women.

In a UCLA study, scientists found that when stressed, the men tended to go off alone or react aggressively ("fight or flight"). The women, on the other hand, tend to their young or gather together to commiserate, cook, and be with others, usually other women ("tend and befriend").

For women, getting together with other women is the healthiest and most effective stress relief. It probably feels particularly good because of all that oxytocin that is released as well. People with high levels of oxytocin are calmer, more relaxed, more social, and less anxious.

Last but not least, an Emory study found that women learn better when surrounded by groups of other women. Our brains even work better when we are together! This is why the Real Estate Investor Goddesses is a community of women learning and growing together. We function better this way.

Sisterhood is good for you!

Having a community of like-minded women is valuable because it can provide you with:

- mentorship

- support

- inspiration

- accountability

- an antidote to the "Good Old Boys Network"

- the "Sassy Sister Network"

When I first got into real estate investment and was surrounded by so many men, I desired to have a community of women that I could support and who could support me as I went into my real estate investing.

The Real Estate Investor Goddesses is the answer to that desire. We are a virtual community (we have members based all over the world), and an off-line community (we also strive to get together in person). Whether near or far, it's a sisterhood that you can rely on to inspire and support you as you go and grow.

Join us at **www.RealEstateInvestorGoddesses.com** to link up to a sisterhood of support for your real estate investing.

***

If you make sure to fill your life with pleasure and sisterhood, and follow your intuitive guidance, your real estate investing will proceed with ease.

The right people will show up, you'll be guided to the right resources, you'll have fun and you'll make money. Doesn't that sound good? It is!

Conclusion

"The only thing standing between me and Greatness is me."
~Woody Allen

OK Goddess, you are ready to go. In this book, you have been given the tools to get started in building your money orchard with real estate investment:

You have been disabused of common myths about real estate.

You were introduced to Real Estate Investing's many benefits.

You learned the 7-Part Real Estate Investor Goddess' Success Framework:

1. the right education

2. the right vision

3. the right team

4. the right market

5. the right property

6. the right financing, and

7. the Goddess Secret Sauce!

Now, the only thing standing between you and greatness is you. :)

You don't have to do this alone though. In fact, you *shouldn't* do this alone. At Real Estate Investor Goddesses, we have put together many tools to support you and to help ensure your success.

Go to **www.RealEstateInvestorGoddesses.com** to access all our tools and services plus support and inspiration from other women investors like you.

I'll see you over there. Don't wait one more second. It's time for us to own the world!

Stay Abundant!

Monick

About the Author

Monick Halm, J.D., CPC is a real estate investor and syndicator with over 12 years of real estate investing experience. She is the co-founder of the Real Estate Investor Goddesses and the host of the Real Estate Investor Goddesses Podcast. She is also a Real Estate Strategy Mentor, certified Money Master Coach, NLP Coach, and Success Coach, interior designer, feng shui expert, bestselling author, speaker, attorney, wife and mother of three amazing kids.

She has made it her mission to empower women to thrive in their lives, families, and careers. She loves connecting with other real estate investing women. You can connect with her on The Real Estate Investor Goddesses web page (**www.RealEstateInvestorGoddesses.com**) or on twitter as @monickpaulhalm.

***

Ready to create lifestyle and financial freedom through real estate? Monick would like to invite you to get started on your real estate investing blue print by signing up for a Real Estate Investor Goddesses Investment Strategy Session where together you will cover any or all of the following:

-your vision and personal investment blueprint
-who should be on your team
-what markets to target
-how to put the Goddess Secret Sauce to work in your life.

Go to **www.RealEstateInvestorGoddesses.com** to book your session!

To order additional copies, including quantity
discounts of

The Real Estate Investor Goddess
HANDBOOK

see below:

TO ORDER PLEASE:

1. Order online www.realestateinvestorgoddesses.com

2. E-mail: info@realestateinvestorgoddesses.com